THE RELATIONSHIP DOCTOR:

DR LUCY ATCHESON'S GUIDE TO
PERFECT RELATIONSHIPS

THE RELATIONSHIP DOCTOR:

DR LUCY ATCHESON'S GUIDE TO PERFECT RELATIONSHIPS

Dr Lucy Atcheson

HAY HOUSE

Australia • Canada • Hong Kong
South Africa • United Kingdom • United States

First published and distributed in the United Kingdom by
Hay House UK Ltd, 292B Kensal Rd, London W10 5BE
Tel.: (44) 20 8962 1230; Fax: (44) 20 8962 1239
www.hayhouse.co.uk

Published and distributed in the United States of America by
Hay House, Inc., PO Box 5100, Carlsbad, CA 92018-5100.
Tel.: (760) 431 7695 or (800) 654 5126;
Fax: (760) 431 6948 or (800) 650 5115
www.hayhouse.com

Published and distributed in Australia by
Hay House Australia Ltd, 18/36 Ralph St, Alexandria NSW 2015
Tel.: 612 9669 4299; Fax: 612 9669 4144
www.hayhouse.com.au

Published and distributed in the Republic of South Africa by
Hay House SA (Pty), Ltd, PO Box 990, Witkoppen 2068
Tel./Fax: 2711 706 6612
orders@psdprom.co.za

Published and distributed in India by
Hay House Publishers India, Muskaan Complex,
Plot No.3, B-2, Vasant Kunj, New Delhi – 110 070
Tel.: (91) 11 41761620; Fax: (91) 11 41761630
contact@hayhouseindia.co.in

Distributed in Canada by:
Raincoast, 9050 Shaughnessy St, Vancouver, BC V6P 6E5
Tel.: (604) 323 7100; Fax: (604) 323 2600

ISBN-10 1-4019-1165-X
ISBN-13 978-1-4019-1165-2

Printed and bound in Great Britain by
TJ International Ltd, Padstow, Cornwall

for Edd

CONTENTS

WHY I WROTE THIS BOOK

HOW OUR RELATIONSHIPS DEFINE US

Our relationships are one of the most important factors in our lives. In fact, to a large extent they define us. Think about it: If you were asked to describe yourself, wouldn't you mention your relationship status? More than that, think back to when you were last happy in your relationship. Didn't it feel like it gave you some protection against the stress and strains of life? That no matter what else was happening in your life, you had this wonderful relationship that you enjoyed?

But if the stresses and strains actually come from within your relationship, what protects you then? Nothing – except your own self-esteem and inner strength – and let's face it, a bad relationship can erode even the strongest person's self-confidence.

So relationships form a huge part of our everyday lives. Just count up the amount of time you spend each day thinking about them. They are invariably one of the first things we ask about when we meet new people and we want to find out more about them. They are the subject of virtually every film, book and song. In fact, they are the topic of so many conversations and theories, sometimes it feels as though they are given too much emphasis, that they have become an obsession. But this has always been the way and will never change, because fundamentally our relationships give us our humanity.

This is one of the reasons why I find working with relationships so incredibly rewarding. There is no getting away from it – when your relationships are going badly, you will be reminded of it at every turn, 100 times a day. So I find saving a relationship, or helping someone to be in the space to have a healthy relationship next time round, an incredibly rewarding experience. A good relationship really can enhance lives.

ALL ABOUT ME

Before I go any further, I should tell you something about myself so you know where I'm coming from. So here are my professional credentials: For the past five years I have been specializing in relationships in my independent practice now in Harley Street, London. Before this I qualified as a counselling psychologist with a Doctorate in Psychotherapeutic and Counselling Psychology from Surrey University. I also have a Masters Degree in the Social Anthropology of Human Development from Brunel University and an Honours Degree in Psychology from Staffordshire University.

I am not listing these qualifications in order to impress you, but rather to let you know that you can trust the advice I give in this book. Gaining these qualifications took seven years of studying, so it has been a long journey for me academically (as well as personally), to reach the stage where I feel qualified enough to write this book on relationships.

And from an academic perspective, getting to this point was not just a case of studying the required books. Becoming a professional psychologist also meant I had to make my own journey of self-discovery and self-development. One of the things it is crucial for a good psychologist to learn is a way of approaching people and the issues they are presenting to you which does not make assumptions or judgements. A good psychologist will learn not to see people as stereotypes, or to apply 'popular thinking', such as assuming there are ever any absolutes in a relationship. So if someone stays with their partner despite that partner being unfaithful, this does not necessarily make the person weak. Equally, we can't assume something would be right for everyone just because it is right for one individual. Advice from friends and family is usually very well meant but often would suit them more than the person they are advising.

Through experience, a good psychologist will learn to look at what people *aren't* saying as much as what they are saying. We develop an instinct for what their true feelings really are and an intuition for what influences their minds. We can do this because people generally are motivated by the desire for the same kind of things, no matter how differently those desires may be expressed. This common ground is vitally important when working through this book, because it means I can guide you to work through issues using your own intuition. Intuition is especially important in relationships as people tend to be very defensive when it comes to examining how they act and behave in their personal lives.

WHY GOOD RELATIONSHIPS ARE SO IMPORTANT

I specialized in relationships not only because I realized how important a healthy relationship is for my clients, but also because I am acutely aware of how important it has been for me. I met my husband when I was 17, and although it was a predictably complicated relationship when we were both adolescents, when we all make everything more complicated than it needs to be, my relationship has since grown into one of the strongest, most protective and most encouraging aspects of my life. In short, I am not sure I would be where I am today without my husband. He has helped me develop the confidence in myself to believe I can do whatever I set my mind to.

However, even the most established of relationships has its minefields, and mine is no exception: I am not holding myself up as an expert in relationships just because I happen to have a good one. I am holding myself up as an expert because I know how to help people work at their relationships and, believe me, I have had to work at mine.

WHY YOU SHOULD NEVER GIVE UP ON YOUR RELATIONSHIPS TOO SOON

All relationships can feel, at times, as though they aren't worth it, and we have all been in the situation when the end has seemed to be firmly in sight. In fact all relationships require constant upkeep and maintenance. It's a truism that keeping a relationship exciting and passionate requires a little work the longer you are together. Relationships are hard work. It takes energy to establish one in the first place and then, when the love is there and the friendship is firmly grounded, it takes even more energy to keep the momentum going. For instance, it is essential to focus on keeping the passion developing – which is ironic, as passion is usually the only thing you *don't* have to focus on in the early days. Then, if you go from couple to family you have to focus on prioritizing the relationship as well as looking after the baby. Or if you go into business together, or one of you decides to take a long-distance job, you will have to adapt together in order to stay together. Basically, as your relationship evolves, the challenges you face will change too.

What a Good Relationship Can Do …

A good relationship can make you feel so positive about yourself, all the hard work will be worth it. We all deserve to feel positive about ourselves at least some of the time, to believe in ourselves and have a sense of self-worth and esteem. And one of the best sources of this confidence is our relationships. I am not saying we can't do this if we are single – of course we can. But when we believe in ourselves and we are with someone who believes in us too, we can feel truly unassailable.

Unfortunately, as is usually the case in this life, what is potentially one of our best sources of support can also, when things go wrong, be the strongest threat to our self-esteem.

What a Bad One Can Do …

An unhealthy relationship can rock even the strongest of us. We have all seen people become shadows of their former selves due to a critical or chaotic relationship. These emotionally shattered people sometimes find their way to consulting rooms where someone like me tries to help them make sense of themselves. But what of all those who cannot afford the time or the money, or who have other reasons for not wanting to see a therapist face to face?

Case Study | Sarah

Sarah and her boyfriend looked like they had it all going for them. They were both in their early forties and had spent their thirties establishing very lucrative businesses that they enjoyed. And they had decided to start trying for a family. On paper, they looked as if they had achieved the coveted position of 'having it all'. The week their fantastic house was finished – after 18 months of renovations to build an über-cool country pile – Sarah's boyfriend proposed. Marriage was something they both felt they were bound to do at some point. Sarah remembers thinking, 'I am the happiest I have ever been,' and was convinced that by the same time the following year she would have everything she ever wanted, including husband and baby.

Sarah was a very strong woman – she had had to be to develop such a successful business in a tricky and highly competitive industry. She genuinely liked the way she looked and took immaculate care of herself. In fact, she had very little time for people who suffered any type of depression.

She was one of the misguided many who thought they should just 'pull themselves together and get on with life'. Then, one week after the engagement proposal, Sarah's boyfriend panicked. He dramatically dumped her and she went into freefall. All of her confidence was shattered, and she simply fell apart. And yes, she ended up on anti-depressants seeking treatment with me.

I am not using this example to say we cannot cope without a partner. As far as I can see, one plus one still equals two, not one. And I personally detest the phrase 'the other half'. So I am not putting across a ridiculous 'smug married' position, all I am pointing out is that I have personally seen even the strongest people, the most secure and confident, seriously shattered by traumatic relationships and break-ups.

HOW I CAME TO WRITE THIS BOOK

In my therapy rooms, I have always felt it important to approach my clients in an integral way. This means that I try and use a combination of all of the main psychological approaches to therapy so that my clients don't all have to fit into one mould or respond to just one type of approach. Instead, I tailor the psychological approach to fit the needs of each individual client. However, over time I realized that these therapeutic processes had some main ingredients that were common to all the clients I was seeing. This gave me the idea of making my relationship psychotherapy accessible to everyone, not just those who can get into a consulting room. So by writing this book, I want to take my therapy out of Harley Street and into everyone's front room.

To this end, I have written this book using the exact same style I adopt in therapy. One great benefit of working through the therapy in a book, rather than in a consulting room, is that my presence is here only in my words; I'm not there in person in the same room as you. So if you or your partner doesn't want to tell a stranger their issues, you or they don't have to – the issues can be worked through in the privacy of your own home.

All the tasks I use are based on solid, proven psychological theory – namely transactional analysis (Berne, 1964)*, interpersonal skills, and psychological communication. But you do not need to study these, or even know anything about them: I have done that for you; after all, that is why couples come and see me. My therapeutic training means I can use my psychological knowledge to understand and fix their relationship and I am able to do the same for you. You can rest assured this book is grounded in psychological theory and practice that have been made as easy and accessible as possible – and fun – for you.

About My Approach

I am not a 'tea and sympathy' psychologist – I don't believe this helps people move on. People don't come to me if they want to wallow endlessly in their woes, they come to me if they want to like themselves enough to beat their woes. Therapy needs to effect change and I don't believe, for example, that clients should be supported to feel

* Berne, E. (1964) *The Games People Play.* New York: Grove Press.

overwhelming self-pity. A bit of self-pity can be healthy, but beyond that what people really need is to be supported while they come to the point of understanding exactly why they've got themselves into this mess in the first place. That means helping them to realize how their early development has affected them, and helping them identify and understand the unconscious patterns they keep repeating again and again.

However, my approach does not dwell too much on your early development. Rather, it concentrates on working in the present, in the here and now, helping you to reject unhealthy patterns and develop a new, more 'authentic' approach to life. With this new approach you will feel much better about yourself, and be able to develop the confidence you need to live a life that is about meeting your needs and being good to yourself.

THE BENEFITS OF WORKING WITH A BOOK

This is why our relationships are so important. And why I have written this book – so that I can help people heal their relationships. And not just in the consulting room. My aim in this book is to literally mirror the therapy process. It will be as though we take the therapy out of the consulting room and into your living room. And the beauty of having the information available in a book means you can work through the therapy in the privacy of your own home.

Why This Book is a Real Alternative to Therapy

There will be many reasons why you are buying this book rather than entering into couple therapy, and this book is not being written as a poor substitute but as a real alternative.

For a start, you may not be able to afford couple therapy. Let's face it, it can be expensive. Alternatively, you may not physically have the time and if you have children it may not be possible to get regular babysitting to enable you to attend weekly therapy. But this should not mean you cannot get the help you need for your relationship – if you can't get to the therapy, let's take the therapy to you.

Also, if you have a very resistant partner they may prefer to do this work through a book rather than face-to-face with a psychologist. It means they don't have to bare their soul to a stranger and they can still get the professional input without the physical presence of the professional. You may also want to try this book first before you make the financial commitment to therapy, and that is also a good idea. But if all goes to plan, this book should be enough to heal your relationship.

TO SUM UP ...

So, to sum up, my relationship therapy – and therefore this book – is based on sound psychological theory. It looks at factors such as how attraction works between people, at personal development within a relationship, at the scripts and roles people unconsciously adopt within relationships, at the unspoken emotional contracts between people.

It will enable you to have deeper self-awareness, and greater empathy and understanding for your partner. It will show you how to recognize how your behaviour affects your own and your partner's thoughts and emotions.

Once you have insight into these, you are well on your way to having as-perfect-as-possible relationships!

CONFIDENTIALITY STATEMENT

I would like to thank all of my clients, as working with them has obviously added to my understanding of psychology and human lives. Whilst it is important in a book like this to illustrate such learning with case studies, I have taken every possible step to protect confidentiality. All names and other identifying features, such as gender, age, relationship status, have been changed; indeed, all of the case studies in this book present composite clients and are not based on one individual or couple. The case studies presented here are typical of many clients and situations, therefore they will resonate with many and are always representative of many and never any one case in particular.

CHAPTER 1

HOW THIS BOOK WORKS:
Taking You Through the Step-by-Step Process

WHAT IS A PERFECT RELATIONSHIP?

This book is a guide to perfect relationships. Perfect relationships sound like a utopian ideal – and surely none of us is realistically going to achieve perfection. But this is not necessarily the case. When I talk about perfect relationships I mean *perfect for you*. Everyone's idea of perfect will be different. Basically, what I mean here is a relationship that makes you happy more often than not and fulfils you more than it drains you, therefore a perfectly balanced relationship. No relationship is going to make you deliriously happy all of the time, but by the same token no relationship should make you sad or worried most of the time. So perfect is happy 80 per cent of the time. And that means truly happy and truly 80 per cent – make sure you are not making excuses for living in a relationship which actually is far more destructive than healthy.

About My Case Studies

Throughout this book I will be drawing on case studies taken from clients I have treated through my practice. However, to preserve confidentiality I have not used people's real names and I've disguised and changed any identifying factors. So if you think you recognize someone, you don't, as I will have changed information about them so they are not recognizable. Indeed, some of my case studies are an amalgamation of two or three couples. The important thing is that the psychological point I am making about their relationship remains the same. The other important point to make about these case studies is that most of the couples are in situations that they could probably have resolved themselves if they had had this book to work through. Most of the case studies illustrate an aspect of the therapy that I then address with the tasks that follow.

Case Study | Rachel and Chris

Rachel and Chris have been together for fifteen years and married for five. They would both describe their relationship as 'perfect for them'. However, others might look at them and think they take too many risks. They could criticize them for living beyond their means, which has put them into debt. Rachel and Chris have also decided they are having too much fun to start a family, which for some seems a selfish position to take.

But the important thing is that their relationship is perfect for them. They actually have a very healthy work/life balance, they value each other and they take care of each other during the good and the bad times. Neither would ever intentionally hurt the other, so they don't believe in having arguments, but of course they disagree from time to time and will debate things. (Debates differ from arguments in that a debate will stay focused on the topic in hand and will not get personal. So a discussion about holiday destinations will not deteriorate into a criticism of one's performance in bed!) (*Much more about this in Chapter 5, looking at the Argument Ruts we get into.*)

On that note, Rachel and Chris try and keep their sex life exciting but also loving. In short, what they do works for them and they would rather be in their relationship and together than doing anything else at any given time. Lastly, and perhaps most importantly, they would not change anything about each other. They are perfect for each other as they are – they fit. Rachel and Chris don't really need to work through this book because at some point in their past they have already worked on their relationship, and they have continued to maintain the changes they made then.

WHAT IS PERFECT FOR YOU?

So the perfect relationship will mean different things for different people. For many it means not being taken for granted. It can mean making sure that both partners put the maximum effort they can into their relationship, because they love their partner more than anyone else in the world and are actively motivated to make sure they never hurt them. And as idealistic as this may sound to you right now, this is an achievable goal for all relationships. An important part of this therapy is for you to have a tangible goal to work towards; an image of what is possible. So take some time now to think about what a perfect relationship – and be realistic! – would mean for *you*.

RELATIONSHIPS SHOULDN'T BE A CONSTANT STRUGGLE

So this book isn't written so much for those lucky enough to be in Rachel and Chris's position – though I'm confident that even the 'happiest' of couples would benefit from reading it and working through the simple tasks I've set out. This book is written for people who are struggling, or have struggled, to maintain happy, healthy adult relationships and who would like to have a relationship pretty similar to that described above.

I would like to stress from the very start that there is absolutely no stigma in admitting that we sometimes struggle in this area – almost all of us will find our relationships a bit of a challenge, for whatever reasons, at some point in our lives. The important thing to remember is that *they do not need to be a struggle*. Your relationship shouldn't make you feel as if you are on a treadmill, continually bogged down by the daily grind of mundane disagreements and hassles.

Remember that You Deserve to Be Happy

So this is your starting point. Try to get away from the conviction that struggle is inevitable because that is what you have always experienced. You deserve to have happy, mutually enriching relationships – and so does your partner. This book will show you how to heal your relationships and make you and your partner happier.

YOU CAN BE YOUR OWN RELATIONSHIP THERAPIST

As I stressed in the Introduction, this guide is entirely based on the relationship therapy I offer the clients who come into relationship therapy with me. Just as I do in therapy, I will guide you through each of the stages and, as I do so, you will see that it is possible for you to be your own relationship therapist. All the counselling you will need you can do by yourself, just by following the step-by-step instructions I describe.

This Book Is For You If …

This book is for anyone struggling with their relationships, regardless of gender, relationship status and sexuality. Just like one-to-one relationship therapy.

You Don't Have to Be Part of a Couple to Benefit

I have also written this book for anyone who isn't currently in a relationship but who wants to understand why their relationships are not working. It will enable you to understand the reasons why your relationships don't work. You will look at the negative patterns you are repeating, what personality type you are and how this impacts your relationship, what personality types you are going for and whether or not they are an entirely healthy choice. By the end of this book you will be in a space to make some major changes to your life and relationships: in terms of approach, attitude, behaviour, and understanding of your personal life.

Your Partner Doesn't Have to Be Involved

This book is also suitable for someone who is in a struggling relationship but whose partner refuses to work through this book with them. If this is your situation, you can work through the book on your own. Doing this will help you to understand your relationship better, understand where it is going wrong, understand yourself more and even understand your partner and why they may be resistant to working things through with you. With this understanding will come the capacity and ability to change these negative patterns and relate to your partner at a level that encourages them to relate to you, rather than to resist.

HOW THIS BOOK CAN HELP – THE STEP-BY-STEP PROCESS

This is how the step-by-step process works, chapter by chapter:

The next chapter, Chapter 2, is all about looking at your relationship – I call it your 'relationship audit'. It focuses on guiding you to identify the main problems in your relationship. It also shows you how important it is to develop your own Emotional Tool Kit, and takes you through your first Task.

Then in Chapter 3 I explain the benefits of committing to an emotional contract – with yourself and your partner, or future partners.

Chapter 4 will look at the question of trust – not necessarily just about fidelity but about *trust* – trust that your partner loves you and that they want the best for this relationship, as much as you do. Trust that this relationship may have a future.

Once you both feel committed to the process and more able to trust each other, in Chapter 5 you will then take a look at the loudest manifestation of your relationship issues – the arguments. Specifically, you will learn how to manage your arguments and use them to resolve, rather than perpetuate, the issues you are both facing.

The next stage in the couple therapy, as set out in Chapter 6, is to try and increase your own self-awareness, as well as develop more empathy for your partner. This will help you understand why you repeat destructive patterns in your relationships – the dynamics of your personality and your partner's can either become complementary or antagonistic, depending on how you interact.

Chapters 7 and 8 focus on helping you to function in a mainly *adult ego state* (I will explain exactly what I mean by this term later in the book). How can you have a healthy adult relationship if you act like a critical parent or a petulant child? At that point, I hope that you will have reached the stage where you are able to have an argument-free, trusting, understanding, committed, and adult relationship.

This experience in itself will do wonders for your self-confidence, but just to be sure you feel better about yourself you will spend a few days, in Chapter 9, working on your self-confidence.

Chapter 10 will help you take a look at your sex life and see how the issues you have been experiencing in your relationship have affected it. Our sex lives are like a mirror to our relationship and are always symptomatic of what is wrong with the relationship.

We end, in Chapter 11, with teaching you how to maintain these changes and setting you up with an Emotional Tool Kit that you will take with you through all the relationships in your life.

WHAT YOU WILL NEED TO DO TO MAKE IT WORK

So that's the basic plan – but how does it actually work? Well, first you, or you and your partner, need to make a commitment.

Making a Commitment

You Will Need 20 Minutes Each Day

It may sound as though all this must take a very long time. Well, it won't. In fact, all you actually need is to spend just 20 minutes a day for the next 30 days on the tasks. I recommend that you read through the whole book first, or at least the whole chapter, before you start working on the tasks in that chapter. This will give you a clear idea of how many days you will need to work through each section.

You may be reading this and thinking, 'If I had 20 minutes a day to focus on my partner or myself, we would not be experiencing difficulties in the first place!' While it's true that we are getting more and more busy and a lot of our incomes are spent on clawing back some time for ourselves, is it really true that you couldn't find just 20 minutes in each day?

Think about it – how many minutes do you spend worrying about your relationship, or thinking about ways to improve it? Or if it is already over, how much time do you spend thinking about what went wrong? Maybe you do this while you are spending time commuting, or you find yourself thinking about it while staring at a computer screen or oven. But you probably *do* think about it.

Stop Obsessing and Start Addressing!

What you are aiming for is to lose all that time you spend letting your problems go round and round your head, obsessing about them without coming to any resolution or insights, and instead use the time to think about your relationship in a focused way. With the result that you resolve issues, learn more about yourself, learn more about your partner, and move the relationship forward, strengthening it as you go. So you ultimately end up with a healthy relationship which requires no concern. After all, what could be a more effective use of your time?

In each of the chapters I will talk through the subject – e.g. arguments – first, with plenty of illustrative case studies, and then set out various tasks for you and your partner to do together, or for you to do alone. These will be the foundations of your relationship therapy.

ARE YOU MOTIVATED?

My therapy focuses on being true to yourself, and to your partner. It will also inspire you to be the best you can be, rather than being what you think others think you should be. In order to achieve all this the old cliché is applicable –

you have to really want to change. They say the old jokes are the best and this one sums it up:

Q: How many psychologists does it take to change a light bulb?

A: One, but the light bulb has to want to change.

If you really want to change your relationship I can help you. Buying this book won't do it alone; you will have to follow the tasks I set out for you throughout the book. Otherwise it would be like buying a diet book, reading it, then putting it back on the shelf without following any of the advice. And then complaining that the diet hasn't worked. This book won't work by osmosis; you will have to follow it step by step. This might sound like an impossible process to you right now, but that's because you can't yet see how you can save your relationship, or even have a healthy one next time round. So leave that part to me for now – that's my job. If you are motivated and follow the tasks, I will do the rest.

Think about it – you have been motivated enough in your desire for change to pick up this book and read thus far. Perhaps you are still standing at the self-help section of the book shop debating whether or not to buy it – asking yourself how you can go from picking up a book to saving your relationship. Well, the answer is that I am confident I can help you save it, but you must also convince yourself you have the inclination to do this. If we were in therapy and you were sitting opposite me now, the first question I'd ask would be, 'What prompted you to come and see me at this time?'

Where Are You At Now?

So ask yourself this question – what made you pick up this book? The answer might be that something small just triggered something inside you. Perhaps someone asked you a simple question, such as, 'How's it going with …?' And you made up an answer, because it suddenly became painfully obvious to you that the relationship was going badly and you were desperately worried it was over.

Or it could be that you are on your own and totally fed up with never getting past the six-month mark in your relationships. Which may be fine in your twenties – in fact serial monogamy definitely can have its benefits – but now in your late thirties or forties it feels a bit lonely, especially when everyone else around you seems to be slinking off into coupledom.

There are a million and one reasons why someone might have felt compelled to pick up this book. Let's face it, I'd never get onto the therapy if we went through every possible permutation. Essentially it doesn't matter what your reasons are, whether they are similar to those suggested above or completely different. If you have picked up this book because you are tired of your relationships failing, and you don't want yet another unhealthy ending, and you don't want to have to go through the ensuing sadness yet again, then this book is right for you.

GETTING YOUR PARTNER INVOLVED

But what about your partner? How will you motivate them into working on your relationship by reading this book and following the tasks? This is a problem to be solved whatever you decide to do; whether you are planning to work through this book, or you are trying to persuade them to come to couple therapy with you.

In my consulting rooms, more often than not it is the female (in straight relationships) that contacts me and sets up the assessment. I then meet the couple and it is often obvious that one half of the couple is there under duress or on a promise! So then it is up to me to assess if the reluctant partner really wants to save their relationship enough to last the course.

Usually I start by asking each of the couple to think about what *their* idea of a good relationship would be, and how it would differ from the one they have now. The answers I get in my therapy tend to focus on behaviour rather than emotions; for example, many say they would like to have fewer arguments. However, even this small statement can be a good enough starting point for the therapy to begin. If your partner would like a more peaceful life, without exhausting arguments, then that is the hook we use to get them involved – that could be one of the incentives to persuading an otherwise reluctant partner to go through this book with you, as one of the key chapters is about escaping the argument rut.

To illustrate this, here's an example of a couple I saw for a while.

Case Study | Isabella and Ty

Ty accompanied his partner Isabella to an assessment. He sat there looking somewhat defensive, as if to say, 'I can't believe I have to be here doing something as ridiculous as telling a stranger about my relationships, and if she asks me about my mother I am leaving ...' Isabella, on the other hand, was clearly ready to invest a great deal in saving her relationship. She was trying to give me all the information she thought I needed, while looking anxiously across at Ty every so often, as though she were worried he would become furious at her, or at me, or just walk out.

Ty was uncomfortable being there, and if you looked at who was making the most effort in the session, he certainly did seem to be less interested in working things out. However, it could also have been that he just did not have the capacity to speak about his emotions as freely as his girlfriend. Let's face it, because of their social conditioning, men are often incapable of, or afraid of, talking about their feelings. So I asked Ty – as I want you to ask your partner – 'What would be your idea of a good relationship?'

Ty managed to tell me that he wished arguments didn't seemingly appear from nowhere and result in huge slanging matches. He reported being really fed up with what he felt were histrionics and unreasonable arguments almost on a weekly basis. However, he also thought that these arguments were now unavoidable and simply symbolized that their relationship was going nowhere and that they were not right for each other.

Like many men in similar situations, Ty was so unhappy with this element of their relationship he could barely verbalize it, and because he couldn't verbalize it he could not see how it was even possible to resolve it. In fact, Ty and Isabella went on to discover that they needed to allow each other to be more authentic in their relationships. That they needed to stop worrying about being true to the other's perception of them and be true to themselves instead. This resulted in a much more contented and relaxed relationship where they each felt genuinely free to be themselves. When they felt authentic they liked themselves in their relationship more, and the knock-on result was that they liked their relationship more too.

ACKNOWLEDGING PROBLEMS CAN BE FRIGHTENING

This is the danger many people fear. You ask your partner to say what is wrong with your relationship and, as this is the first time they have really addressed the problems, they suddenly seem to be much more real and tangible and overwhelming.

This is what I do in my therapy: I acknowledge that the couple have things they would like to change and I reassure them that simply by identifying them they are now one step closer to actually resolving them. I stress that there is no need to end the relationship yet. I encourage them to work through the course, and if things still haven't changed at the end of the therapy, then and only then it may be time to call time on the relationship. This may sound like the death knell for your relationship but it's not. Actually trying to change things gives your relationship a much greater chance of survival than keeping your head buried in the sand.

IT ONLY TAKES ONE MONTH ...

Working through the tasks set out in this book will take approximately one month, with tasks taking about 20 minutes a day. That is all. So if your partner – or you – is reluctant to commit that kind of time, take a moment to think about it. What could seem like a hassle for just 20 minutes a day, over the course of just one month, will actually lead to a much happier time of it for the rest of your lives. And if you look at it like that, it will suddenly seem like a much more attractive, almost an irresistible, proposition.

TO SUM UP ...

Whether you are going through this step-by-step process on your own or with your partner, you will come out at the end understanding why your relationships struggle and how you can break these destructive patterns. This book is for anyone who would like to learn more about having healthy, happy relationships, and who is willing to put just a little time and effort into doing so.

DO YOU NEED THIS BOOK?
Your Relationship Audit

It is really hard to admit to ourselves when our relationship is in trouble. Refusing to admit that we have made mistakes is a natural human characteristic – it is called denial. We deny issues to ourselves in order to protect ourselves, as if we believe that if we do not acknowledge that the painful or tricky stuff even exists, it can't hurt us. Of course we know deep down that nothing could be further from the truth. Have you ever heard the old saying, 'Least said, soonest mended'? That saying is based on denial and to my mind is terribly inaccurate. I actually think the only situation where this rule can be applied is when you are very drunk! Then I do advocate saying nothing, as whatever you say is likely to come out in a hugely exaggerated way, and may well give you the horrors when you wake up the following morning with not just a hangover but oodles of regret over what you said …

Unfortunately, denial does not really protect us. All it achieves is that we end up like an ostrich with our head in the sand. Meanwhile, the issue we are trying to avoid looms ever larger and gets more and more complicated the longer it is left, unresolved, to fester. So now be honest with yourself – you must have at least an inkling that something is wrong with your relationship or you would not have picked up this book and be reading this now. But how do you go from having a nagging feeling of uneasiness to making a decision to do something about it?

To identify if your relationship struggles, first ask yourself the following questions:

DO YOU NEED TO CHANGE YOUR RELATIONSHIP?

Think about your relationship for a moment and ask yourself:

Was there a time when your relationship was better than it is now? If so, how was it different?

Here are some thought guides:

- Did you feel more valued by your partner?
- Currently, do you ever feel like you come second, or worse, in your partner's priorities to … golf, work, alcohol, friends, family, PlayStation … (adapt as appropriate)?
- Currently, do you feel more relaxed away from your partner than with them?
- Has more than a month passed since you last had sex and is there no real reason for this?
- Do you feel a general sense of unease about your relationship (you probably do, or you wouldn't have picked up this book in the first place)?

- Do you find yourself feeling that it would be better if only ... your partner grew up, got a promotion, you looked different, the family butted out more, the kids were older ... (again, fill in as appropriate)?

It could be all or any of these things, or some totally different issues – the list could literally be endless. If you are struggling to think about what needs to change or what could be wrong between you then try this:

Imagine you are on a date like the ones you used to go on, or even go out together, just the two of you on a date similar to those you had in the first throes of passion, and ask yourself, 'What is different about us emotionally, and how has the way we relate to each other changed?'

We are not aiming to pinpoint exactly what is wrong with your relationship at this stage; we are simply trying to decide if the feelings of unease merit doing something about fixing your relationship. I firmly believe that most uneasy feelings are warning signs of danger yet to come, a bit like intuition. Think about it – how many times have you heard a friend who has just suffered a break-up say, 'I knew something was wrong but did not want to think about it'? Having regrets over not doing anything while the relationship was breaking down is very hard to bear, so if you do have the feeling that all is not well in your relationship don't stick your head in the sand – communicate properly with your partner now. With the help of this book, it will be a case of 'effectively said, soonest mended'. Don't add regret to the list of psychological issues you are trying to resolve.

Don't Give Up on Your Relationship Too Soon

Perhaps you feel certain your relationship already has ended. Well, most people come to me in that position – thinking their relationship has ended and that they are just checking whether or not they are really doing the right thing by breaking up, perhaps for the sake of the kids or whatever. And often I will fix their relationship. So there is no reason why this can't work for you. Work through this book and *then* decide.

Case Study | Mia and Tom

Mia and Tom had been together for four years but they both felt deep down that for the last two their relationship had been purely perfunctory – more of a habit than anything else. They had well and truly got stuck on a treadmill. Their relationship and their sex lives were very routine – both fitted around their work lives. Interestingly, on paper they looked like they were succeeding in life as they both had good jobs and were being promoted at fast-track speed. They had bought a town house in a really fashionable and fun part of London, although, as it transpired, they never got to enjoy their area together as a couple, as they were always working or out with other people. On paper they seemed to do lots together, but in practice this actually amounted to little more than going to the gym most mornings at 6am before work, then running on adjacent treadmills while listening to their iPods. Not exactly conducive to conversation!

They saw their friends most Saturday nights and prided themselves on their social life, which was based around drinking a great deal and spending Sunday 'in recovery'. They had stopped asking themselves what they wanted, and did things because they were in their diary, rather than because they wanted to. They had fun when their evenings were mixed with the right amount of alcohol and they had good sex if it was mixed with the right sex aid, but never did they really engage with each other or themselves. Until one morning they woke up and thought that although they were good friends (Although were they? Isn't friendship based on sharing?) and loved each other, it was undoubtedly true that they were not *in love* with each other.

So they decided they would see a relationship specialist, as they thought that that is what you do before you end a relationship. So even their decision to come and see me was a perfunctory task — like most of the things in their life it had been put down in their diary, therefore they came.

During the therapy, they told me that although they loved each other they were no longer *in love* with each other. When I asked them to clarify this, they couldn't. (Like most people, they had adopted this phrase as a blanket expression to explain all their relationship problems. But before you ever say it, you really should ask yourself what you actually mean by it. What is really missing?)

This was exactly what I asked Mia and Tom, and thinking about how they felt rather than ignoring their feelings was the very first step they took to healing their relationship.

This did not happen magically overnight, it took work from both of them, but it stemmed from the tiniest of first steps. And as you work through the book, we will follow this couple through their journey, as you go through yours.

In the case of Mia and Tom, their issues were based on the fact that they never really experienced, or focused on, each other. They just sort of co-existed side by side and this even extended to their physical relationship. They never really touched each other, instead they had what they described as really exciting sexual experiences using sex aids or dressing up in rubber. However, just as they were doing in life, so in sex. They had shifted the focus from each other onto the aids or the outfits. They experienced pleasure individually, but with a barrier between them. They managed the task at hand in so far as they both experienced orgasm, but they didn't manage to build any emotional and sexual bonds between them.

Just as it is important to get the balance right in life, between work and relationships and so forth, so balance is key within the relationship too. Some sexual experimentation is always good but the key word is *some* – you don't want every sexual experience between you and your partner to be based on plastic or rubber or something else. Experiencing just the two of you connecting is also vital.

YOUR INPUT IS ESSENTIAL TO THE PROCESS

This guide does not just give you the theory and then leave you to put it into action. It gives you step-by-step, practical tasks to do on a daily basis. This means that you not only understand the theory behind why you need to make these changes in your life, but you also know *how* you can make them. The practical exercises make the help direct, not vague.

Because *you* have to work through the exercises, you have to do the thinking, and when you have followed the relevant tasks, you will be the one to find the right answers, the answers that are specific for *your* relationship. This is because your issues will not be the same as those for every other member of the population – that is just not possible.

By the time you have completed your month-long journey you will be well on the way to developing your *Emotional Tool Kit* to help you find and maintain perfect relationships.

✎ BUILDING UP AN EMOTIONAL TOOL KIT

Our Emotional Tool Kits are the invisible understanding and techniques we carry around with us to help us deal with any stressful situation. The best tool kits help us do this while remaining authentic and true to ourselves. Throughout this book the tasks I set out are developed specifically to help you build up your own Emotional Tool Kit, one you can call on whenever you find yourself in an emotionally challenging situation.

For instance, this Tool Kit will stop you from acting very calmly and rationally one second, then flipping into a screaming child the next, in response to a stressful situation. We build up these Tool Kits primarily through understanding our emotions – a process which is not as simple as it sounds, but which I facilitate through the Tasks in this book. Once you have more understanding about what makes you tick, you can store the techniques detailed in this book as Tools to help you maintain your balance whatever life and love throw at you.

Whenever you see the symbol ⚒ throughout the book, I am discussing techniques which will be an invaluable addition to your Emotional Tool Kit. Ultimately, whenever you are in a stressful situation you will be able to pick whichever tool you think will be most effective to help you deal successfully with the problem at hand.

What Will You Need?

So, now you have decided you want to get the help from this book, what exactly will you need to do? First, there are a few practical props you will need:

Time

- You will need just a little time – most of the tasks will take roughly 20 minutes per day. The only exceptions are on Day 2 and Day 13, for which you will need about two and a half hours each day. This may sound like a heavy commitment at first but you can make it fun. A lot of my clients do these tasks over dinner, so that they enjoy what they are doing and it becomes real quality time spent together. If you decide to do this, limit the wine to a bottle between you or the tasks might not go as well as they should, or may even be abandoned altogether!

A Notebook

- You will need a notebook handy for doing the tasks. Mainly we will be dealing with emotions, so it is your Emotional Toolbox that we will be working on. We will tap into the rational, loving, calm, adult, grounded, self-protective emotions that you innately possess and build them up for you.

I do suggest that you start on a Saturday, or another day when you do not work. This is important as you need to allow yourself the time to start properly, in order not to set this process up to fail. Furthermore, Day 2 and Day 13 are very intensive days, where we deal with a situation in one go. It would be possible to break this part of the therapy down, but due to the nature of the psychology behind these emotions it works best if we work through the tasks one after the other for maximum impact and change. These two sections will need about two and a half hours, so make sure you set aside the time in advance.

WILL IT WORK FOR ME?

This guide really can work for anyone. But if you are still unsure as to whether or not it is for you, try the following task to give you an idea of how simple, but effective, the process can be.

This task is typical of most of the other tasks in terms of the amount of thought and self-awareness you will need. As I stated in the earlier chapters, I am starting from the premise that you have not been through therapy before, therefore I will not expect you to be well-versed in psychology or to be familiar with psychological terms – this guide will teach you those.

✎ YOUR TASKS FOR THE RELATIONSHIP AUDIT
🕐   These Tasks will take 1 day.

DAY 1

👥 👤 *Couples and individuals do the same task below:*

Simply list all of the issues you feel you have in your relationship. Here are some possible examples:

- Arguments

- Feeling undervalued

- An unfulfilling sex life

- Issues regarding trust

- Paranoia about exes

- Insecurity about how your partner feels about you

- Fear of being left

- Fear the relationship won't progress to the next stage – for example, moving in together, starting a family and so on

- Feeling like you take all the responsibility for financial matters and so forth.

Throughout the book, we will work through the underlying factors causing the issues you have listed. For now, keep the list you have made. At the end of the book I will ask you to look at it again, to check we have done everything we need to.

Even if you only have a few issues you should do this. There is no minimum or maximum number you need to have to benefit from the therapy. But by the end of the journey you should have resolved these issues in your relationship, or, if you are doing this on your own, you should be ready to have a relationship without repeating the same destructive pattern.

WELCOME TO YOUR EMOTIONAL JOURNEY

By completing this basic first task, you have just taken the first steps on your journey to healing your relationship. Identifying the problems is the first step on the road to resolving them. You are no longer in denial, with your head buried in the sand, but you have begun to engage with your problems. By acknowledging these issues and identifying them you are beginning to shape the way you will resolve them. This is sometimes the hardest thing to do, and if you've managed to do this, you can certainly do the rest of the therapy.

To illustrate this point I am going to return to Mia and Tom, the couple we will be following throughout the book as they work through the different stages of the therapy.

Case Study | Mia and Tom

Mia and Tom, as I have already said, did not recognize their relationship was dying until it was almost dead. When they came to see me in my consulting room they were really just looking for clarification that they were right in their decision to split up. Earlier on in the chapter I told you how I had asked them each to think about what was wrong with their relationship. They received this information with blank looks at me, as though I were really naïve. Surely I could see that the relationship had just fizzled out through no fault of their own? What they weren't recognizing was that relationships never just fizzle out by themselves, we always end them, even if it is simply by massive amounts of doing nothing to try and fix them.

When forced, Mia and Tom were able to make their lists of what went wrong, but in order to do this they first had to go through how they spent their time. It is often the case that when someone is having a really hard time accessing their feelings, it helps to have them come at their feelings via their actions. So, instead of asking them what was wrong in their relationship, I simply asked them what they *did* in their relationship. I literally asked them each for a sort of timetable of their days, and then asked them what time that left for themselves or each other.

Through making this list, Tom realized that he did not feel valued in the relationship, he just felt like he was acting out a role, a part in a play. He realized this when he identified that all his time was spent fulfilling tasks. Mia realized that what was wrong for her was that she felt Tom did not make her feel special. Again, she only came to realize this through talking about what she did hour by hour, day by day, and how she felt about it. This led her to the realization that she only felt good about herself when she had achieved something at work. In fact, Mia and Tom both got their self-esteem from work, rather than each other. So they then added these issues to their lists:

- Don't feel special

- Feel like I'm acting out the role of partner, not being Tom-the-partner

- Feel stuck in a routine (they both realized they felt like this as they talked, and each week merged into one massive timetable)

- We never stop to think about how we feel

- There's no spark or excitement in our sex life – or even just in life in general.

Make a Timetable of Your Average Day

It took a lot of cajoling to get this list out of them. So if, like Mia and Tom, you are struggling to identify your issues, make a timetable of what you do hour by hour, day by day, as a rule. Then ask yourself how that makes you feel, and you will start to see what is missing from your life. For instance, it could be excitement that is missing from your daily life. And this will give you the clue as to what is missing in your relationships.

TO SUM UP ...

So now you have worked through the first chapters and completed your first tasks, you are well on your way. You will have started to identify precisely what is wrong with your relationship and how you are going to start to change it. You have started to think about building up your own Emotional Tool Kit for dealing with difficult situations. In fact you now have everything you need to kick-start the whole healing process.

Welcome to your own self-help therapy!

CHAPTER 3

YOUR EMOTIONAL CONTRACT
Giving You the Confidence to Change

If you've come this far, by now you will have made the decision to start working on your relationship. Having completed your first task, you probably feel confident that you'll be able to work through the step-by-step processes in this book. Congratulations! Making this kind of decision is undoubtedly a wise move, but it is also a very brave one. Emotionally, you may feel that finally admitting to yourself and your partner that something is very wrong is taking a huge emotional risk. In fact, as I explained in the previous chapter, it would be far riskier to just leave your relationship to founder without any help. Admitting that something is wrong and needs fixing is the essential first step in any process involving change.

FEELING COMFORTABLE WITH THE PROCESS

Now you need to give yourself the best possible chance of success. This best chance comes from making the journey you are about to embark on as non-threatening as possible. We always feel the least threatened when we feel the most comfortable. So let's help you now to feel as comfortable as you can in your relationship, given the circumstances, by looking at how you start developing the trust between you. To establish the necessary levels of trust in order to look realistically at your relationship, you will need to agree on an emotional contract.

YOUR CONTRACT TO COMMUNICATE EFFECTIVELY

The ability to communicate effectively with your partner is the most important component in your Emotional Tool Kit.

Without it, you will not be able to discuss your relationship constructively. This contract is vitally important if your therapy is to be effective. We will be referring back to it during all the tasks, so this contract should become like a new mantra for both of you, one that reminds you both how to listen to each other.

Why Mantras Work

A mantra is something that you repeat over and over to yourself in your head. After a while this means that the information will be always readily available to you. Unconsciously, soon you will be implementing the new thinking all the time without even realizing it, just because you have been reminding yourself of it on a conscious level several times a day.

Even if you are doing this by yourself, this emotional contract is really important. Very often, people do not actually listen to what they are really feeling, what is going on inside themselves. Not admitting something, even to yourself, is another form of denial. So if you are working through this book as an individual, your new mantra should be to listen to your own thoughts first and foremost, and follow your trains of thought through to their conclusions. However painful this process is, it must be completed, rather than rushing on to the next subject, and burying any misgivings.

These next points to help you communicate better are also invaluable elements of your Emotional Tool Kit.

✎ START LISTENING

The basis of this contract is that you agree to really communicate with each other, and therefore really *listen* to each other. This, as with most things in life, is psychologically more complicated than it sounds. Often we think we are listening when in fact we are not – we are taking it in turns to have an audience. Think about the last time you were part of a group discussion. Was everyone genuinely listening to one another, or were they using each other to sound off? As someone else talked, were you listening to them or were you just thinking about what you were going to say in response? Doing this is not the same as active listening. It may sound ridiculous, but listening properly takes training. However, I am going to give you a very quick crash course that will enable you to listen properly while you work through this book. Ultimately, you can't establish trust until you have established rapport, and in order to do that on a deep level, you need to really listen.

So the first and foremost item on your contract is to agree to really listen to each other.

THE SIX LISTENING RULES

Real listening, according to McKay, Davis and Fanning (1983)*, is based on the motivation and intention to do six things:

- Understand someone
- Empathize with someone
- Enjoy someone
- Learn something
- Share with someone, as in share their experience by really hearing about it
- Give help or support.

Real intention to do the above things does not come from wanting to look good. It does not mean *looking* as though you are interested. Save that for your boss or someone you want to impress, but don't try it on with your partner while you are working through this book. Real intention also does not come from wanting to placate your partner – for instance, secretly thinking, 'If I look like I am doing this for 20 minutes, I can watch TV in peace afterwards.' Real intention comes from genuinely wanting to engage with the above six factors. So reflect for just a moment. Can you face sharing a lifetime with someone you can't share real communication with?

Let's start with a list of things that are real barriers to listening.

* McKay, M., Davis, M. and Fanning, P. (1983) *Messages: The Communications Skills Book*. Oakland, CA: New Harbinger Publications.

YOU'RE NOT LISTENING WHEN YOU ARE ...

Comparing

This is when you constantly compare what your partner says with how you feel. Instead of doing this, try to listen first and then filter the information and compare. Otherwise you will make assumptions about what they are saying and not really hear their point.

Case Study | Mia and Tom

Tom started discussing how he felt under pressure in the relationship. Rather than letting him have his say, Mia immediately butted in with all the things *she* had to do. This resulted in a 'poor me' scenario, with each of them trying to outdo the other in terms of how bad they had it, as if they were in competition with each other to try and win sympathy.

When this happens, neither partner will really hear the other. All they will be thinking about is how hard they have it, while getting ever angrier with the situation and with the other person. Both positions become more entrenched, with each partner convincing themselves that they really are the wronged party. You don't need a doctorate in psychology to work out that all this is just point scoring, and bears no resemblance to real listening at all.

An example of dialogue from this case study follows:

Tom: Sometimes I feel undervalued, as though we are not really in a proper relationship with each other and ...

Mia: How he can say he is undervalued is beyond me! I do everything to make his life easier – in fact I wish he would do half as much for me!

Mind Reading

I am not suggesting we all have psychic abilities. Far from it. But we can think we know our partner so well that we assume we know what they are about to say. Maybe sometimes they do say certain things over and over again. If this is the case, stop. Don't make assumptions. Listen again. If they are harping on about something, it is probably because nothing is changing. Maybe they do appear to be saying it numerous times, but be honest with yourself – are you really hearing what they are saying and taking it on board?

Rehearsing Your Point

Like barristers in a courtroom, neither of you is really hearing what your partner is saying if you are only planning your response while they talk. You simply can't be really listening if you are too busy thinking about how to answer them. If your partner gets cross if you don't reply to them immediately, remind them of this: A considered response is better than an immediate response. An immediate response often suggests response planning while they talked.

Filtering

As I discussed in the last chapter, we all have a tendency to deny things at times. Similarly, we all have a tendency to 'filter out' a lot of what we hear in order to hold on to our state of denial and ignorance. But, filtering what you hear is a huge threat to effective communication, and therefore to your relationship. If you only hear what you want to hear and only see what you want to see, how can you both have a mutually satisfactory relationship? If whole chunks of your communication are being denied and ignored, it is simply not possible. So actually listen to every word your partner says. Follow *their* words inside your head, not your own.

Judging

This is a huge block to couples talking and listening to each other. Instead of listening, you judge. This means that you evaluate what they are saying rather than listening to them speak. What does this do? It cuts them off so they become afraid to express their opinions or they lack the motivation to try and talk to you. No-one deserves to either judge or be judged. What makes you think you have the right to judge? Are you perfect? Of course not. Being judgemental will stop you from being someone others want to share stuff with. And you can't have a happy relationship unless you are sharing things together.

Placating

We have all, at one time or another, placated ourselves. Perhaps we have been worrying about something and, before we allow ourselves to even finish the thought, we are already off thinking that probably things aren't as bad as we first thought. While this kind of thinking has its uses, it's not a good idea to do it too often, either in relationships, or to ourselves. Being placatory is only really appropriate at the end of a train of thought, or, if you are doing this with your partner, at the end of the topic you have been talking about – not before. Trying to placate someone before they've even finished what they are saying often sends out the message that they are being silenced, or patronized, rather than being given genuine reassurance.

YOUR CONTRACTUAL AGREEMENT

As well as properly listening to each other, you and your partner undertake to agree on the following:

Respect Each Other's Pace

You and your partner may want to work through the therapy at different paces, so you will now try and reach a compromise on your collective pace. You will agree not to hurry each other up unnecessarily, or ridiculously hinder the process.

Respect Each Other's Confidentiality

You will both agree to work at this confidentially. You can't encourage and support each other to work through these private, personal issues if you feel that the other is going to run and tell their friends exactly what has happened after each session.

Respect Each Other's Commitments

You will both set aside a reasonable amount of time to do this together, without forcing the other or feeling forced into something yourself.

Respect Each Other's Opinions

You will not give each other guilt trips over something that may have been said during this self-therapy process, or hold their answers, or their reactions to the tasks, against them.

Don't Start Any Guilt Trips

This is one area where you really have to watch yourselves. If you were seeing me as a psychologist, it would my job to help you avoid this particular minefield. What I mean by 'guilt tripping' is the habit of holding what the other has said against them. Women are particularly adept at doing this; we've all had the 'Three months ago you said …' conversation, and miraculously, a women will remember that conversation almost exactly word for word.

A psychologist would stop you from going down the, 'But you said …' route because it effectively silences further communication. If your partner feels that you are likely to use what they say against them, then logically they will come to the conclusion that maybe it's best if they don't say anything at all. The whole point of this book is to free up communication and thought. If you want the therapy to succeed it is vital you don't throw your partner's point of view back in their face.

The best way to stop yourself doing this is to remember that you need to free up communication, not smother it. So you really will be shooting yourself in the foot if you hold them negatively accountable for all they say. Instead, appeal to your logical self and don't allow yourself to do this. It's time to exercise some self-control.

It will really help if you both agree from the outset not to do this. Then when one of you starts to wander into this minefield with a 'Well, you said ...', the other needs to exercise self-control and remind you that you agreed not to do this. It takes a lot of self-control to keep reminding someone, rather than just reacting and entering into the issue. And remember to remind in an adult, non-judgemental way. That means not yelling, 'You bitch, I knew you'd throw that back in my face!'

Be Realistic

Be fair to each other when agreeing the above points. Don't expect miracles and don't try to bully each other into doing things. Be firm and stress to each other that pledging to support each other while working through this book is necessary if your relationship is going to survive. You both need to be straight with each other about how much time you are willing to give to try and prioritize your relationship and the work you need to do to improve it.

Be Positive

Once you have worked through these points together and reached an agreement, acknowledge that you have both done well, that you are both working to improve the relationship. Perhaps at this stage you are putting different levels of commitment in, but this may change. The main thing is that there is still an ember keeping the fire of the relationship alight.

Agreeing this 'relationship contract' together may be the first adult compromise you have reached together in a while. Hopefully, if you follow this book successfully through to the end – and there is no reason now why you shouldn't – it will be the first of many.

✎ YOUR TASKS FOR THE EMOTIONAL CONTRACT

🕐 These tasks will take 1 day.

DAY 2

You Both Agree to Sign Up to the Counselling Contract

👥 *Couple's Task*

If you are doing this as a couple, your next task is to sit down together and make an undertaking to each other that you will follow these guidelines at all times.

👤 *Individual's Task*

If you are doing this on your own, then make a guarantee to yourself that you will complete this process.

Your Guarantees

• You will both try to work through all the stages of this book.

- You will both set aside just 20 minutes a day to complete the tasks. (As mentioned above, there are two days when a longer stretch of time will be needed.)

- During this process, neither of you will be judgemental towards the other. You know you have different opinions on certain things, or you wouldn't be having these troubles now. But you are going to make a concerted effort to respect those differences. You may not always agree with each other, but you undertake not to belittle or laugh at the other's point of view.

TO SUM UP ...

So, now you have made an emotional contract either with yourself or with your partner, and you understand that the key tools in your Emotional Tool Kit are to listen and to communicate.

Now let's move to the next chapter to address the first big issue I usually come across – trust.

CHAPTER 4

BUILDING TRUST
The Essential Foundation for a Happy Relationship

In the last chapter you drew up a contract to help you communicate with each other and trust each other enough to work on the therapy together. Now we shall look at the whole area of trust in the broader sense of your relationship.

A relationship without trust is a breeding ground for insecurity and paranoia. Trusting someone and feeling trusted can make you feel good about yourself, your partner and your life in general. However, trust is fragile and once it has been broken it takes a lot of work to get it back again.

Even trust that has been betrayed in a previous relationship can impact massively on your current relationship. So why does betrayal cause this carry-over effect? Partly because people often blame themselves for their partner's infidelity. So many times I've heard phrases like, 'If I had been more perfect, they would not have needed to look elsewhere!' Of course this is wrong, but it seems to be almost inevitable where trust has been broken.

The 'Victim Effect'

In therapy this constant blaming of the self is known as the 'victim effect'. This happens when it becomes too frightening to think that you have no control over your partner cheating on you, or otherwise betraying your trust. Therefore you try and come up with a reason for their betrayal over which you can have some semblance of control. That's why I have often heard the refrain: 'If I am perfect, no-one will cheat on me again.' You convince yourself that if you strive to be perfect you can control the fidelity of your relationship and therefore also the trust.

This is not true. In order to have a trusting relationship, you both need to be committed to the cause. Obviously, it is possible that you could have done something to contribute to a partner's infidelity, but that doesn't mean you should take all the blame – nor does it mean you can take all the responsibility for preventing their wanderlust in the future.

Trust is also one of those emotions that you can only receive if you give. Your partner needs to be able to trust you, so you have to trust them too. By definition, trust is not complete if it is only one-sided. Furthermore, a relationship without trust is not really worth having as you will never have inner peace while you are in a paranoid place.

ADDICTED TO INSECURITY

Some people actually become addicted to insecurity and paranoia and actively seek out relationships where activities like checking the calls made on their partner's mobile is the norm. If you are doing this, you need to ask yourself what this insecurity is actually giving you:

- Does this insecurity over your relationship distract from problems elsewhere in your life?

- Is it a rather complicated way of feeling that your relationship is fulfilling, as it literally takes up all of your time, albeit in an unhealthy way?

- Or is it because you struggle to believe anyone could possibly stay faithful to you, either because of previous heartbreak or a low self-image?

If any of these are true, you definitely need to work on building the trust in your relationship, as all of the above situations are untenable in the long term.

TRUST IS NOT JUST ABOUT FIDELITY

Of course there are many ways trust can be broken in a relationship. You can distrust your partner over their fidelity, or over betrayal in any other form. All are equally damaging and can eat away at your relationship if you let them.

Case Study | Mark and Sally

Mark married Sally after four years of dating. Before marriage their relationship was reportedly very calm and lots of fun. It was Sally's second marriage – her first had lasted for under a year. Mark really struggled with this fact. He was scared because he felt Sally had walked away from her first marriage at the first sign of trouble, and worried she would do the same with him. However, at the first sign of trouble she stayed and tried to work through it. This should have been enough for him to recognize how much she loved him and was committed to their relationship, but there was still a thorn in his side – her friendship with her first husband.

Sally was an empathic wife but naïvely insensitive. She referred to her first husband by a pet name out of habit, although she had no feelings for him any more. Further, she met with him for lunches where they caught up on each other's lives, which in Sally's case included sharing details of her relationship with Mark. Sally was naïve because she thought Mark knew how much she loved him and was therefore secure in their relationship. She believed he wouldn't be threatened by her friendship with her first husband, who she thought had moved on as much as she had. She believed her first husband just wanted her to be happy, just as she wished that for him. Mark tried to be understanding, but let's face it, for most this would be hard to tolerate quietly.

The consequence of all this was that she was making Mark insecure by not being more sensitive to his misgivings about her friendship with her ex. This caused him to start to distrust her. This was exacerbated by the fact that her ex gossiped about what she told him, all of which eventually got back to Mark. Mark, understandably, was distraught that Sally had been talking about their relationship problems with her ex. Ultimately, Sally had set herself up to be distrusted even though her intentions were totally honourable, which made her feel very unfairly treated and angry. Moreover, Mark felt extremely wronged, as he did not consider himself overly insecure, which he wasn't.

This case study demonstrates three very important things:

1. That trust within a relationship needs to be continuously protected.

2. That the assumptions others can make about your intentions must be taken seriously and are often as important as the reality.

3. That if you don't communicate clearly in sensitive situations you could make it look as though you are betraying your partner, even if you are not. The only solution is transparent adult communication.

Finding Solutions

Sally needed to explain to Mark why she wanted to stay friends with her ex. In fact, it transpired that this is all they ever should have been, because they never really had passion together as a couple. So a platonic friendship between them was totally possible on her side. As far as she was concerned, Mark was the love of her life, but Sally had never really told him that forcibly enough. Ironically, her ex did know this and was a bit hurt that she felt this, so Sally needed to be on her guard not to give him information that could undermine her current relationship. It seemed that the ex felt more for her than she did for him, so although a careful social friendship was appropriate, an emotionally intimate one was not.

Once the seeds for mistrust had been sown, Sally needed to repair matters with Mark and explain why she had talked to other people about their problems. In trying to get support, albeit from the wrong source, she was guilty of being naïve rather than of betrayal. Mark needed to forgive her, while Sally needed to show him she could have a more appropriate relationship with her ex, in the form of a catch-up once or twice a year, but no more. And perhaps she even needed to phase these out too, if her ex did not move on with his own life. Plainly, Mark was her present and therefore needed to come first in her emotional loyalty.

As you can see, there are consequences of not protecting the trust in your main relationship, which always outweigh the benefits of any platonic friendship.

Other people are not always the cause of loss of trust. We can lose trust in a relationship when no-one else is involved.

Case Study | Jack and Daniel

Jack and Daniel had been together for three years. They got together because at first they seemed to complement each other. Jack brought excitement to the relationship and Daniel brought stability, and initially it seemed a very good mix. But cracks began to appear when Daniel began to feel he was not 'interesting' or, to use that awful phrase, 'cool enough' for Jack's friends. So, as with many insecure people, he tried to do something to make himself 'cooler'. This was not a conscious decision – he told himself he just wanted more fun, but unconsciously he desperately wanted to fit in. Jack did not see this insecurity as he thought Daniel was just wonderful. Daniel was too insecure to realize he was adored for being himself and had no reason to change.

In order to fit in more, and be a bit wilder, he started taking cocaine. And soon the odd line on a Friday night after work became a line every time he went out, until he was reaching for the powder and the rolled-up £20 note four or five times a day. At this point he stepped over the line from 'acceptable' party-scene use to habit. The cruel double standard that exists around this meant that while people had wanted to party with him when he was doing the occasional line, once he was snorting coke in order to get out of bed he was seen as a failure.

And Jack was no different. He became angry because he was left distraught at apparently being replaced by a drug in his partner's passions. He stopped seeing Daniel as a fun person to be with and started seeing him as an addict and a drain on their finances. Four grams of cocaine a day does not come cheap. He also felt he had betrayed his trust as he started to lie about the frequency with which he was doing the drug, as all drug addicts do. And Daniel himself also felt betrayed, as Jack was not supportive in helping him to stop his habit, but simply condemning of his condition.

Both had their points. But because they refused to look at how they had both let the trust slip away from their relationship, they did end up seperating, with both feeling well and truly let down. Trust in a relationship is never killed by just one person. If you are the injured party, however wronged you feel, discussing your feelings with your partner should help you understand what is happening to your relationship before it reaches breaking point.

RELATIONSHIPS WITH A SERIAL CHEAT

Some people need to feel more powerful in a relationship. Some even cheat on their partner in order to feel they have the upper hand. This is extremely cold-hearted – basically these people are using sexual conquests to boost their ego and feed their need for power. If you are attracted to this kind of person, then you need to ask yourself why. Why do you use relationships to harm yourself? Why do you choose a lover who will continue to chip away at your already fragile self-esteem?

If you are the serial cheat, then you need to really think about what you are doing. Using people does not give you power, it just makes you someone who is not worthy of respect. If you really felt as positive about yourself as you try and pretend, then you would not need to use sex as a dubious weapon against your low self-esteem. In fact, making yourself someone who is unworthy of respect is only going to chip away at your fragile self-esteem anyway, however much denial you try to hide behind.

Case Study | Nick

Nick had been very promiscuous and unfaithful to his partners for as long as he had been having relationships. Indeed, as a young man this had made him extremely popular – it meant his friends always followed him to whichever nightspots he went to as they knew he would help them meet lots of women. So as a teenager this behaviour earned him a modicum of respect. Nick felt empowered by this respect and the fact that women were attracted to him, but deep down he was very insecure and soon started to need to get his 'fix' of women finding him attractive. So he began to become the type of man that would flirt with anyone, even his friend's girlfriends, and his wife's friends.

After a while, this behaviour became a running joke. Those friends who had once looked up to him for his 'pulling power' now made fun of him, scorning his continual flirting and serial cheating. The very behaviour that Nick believed would bring him respect among his peers was, in fact, now making him look like a clown. However, if he had stopped at just flirting he would have been teased but not disliked. But his almost pathological cheating meant he was now actively despised by those who had once cared about him. He cheated on his wife so much that she eventually divorced him.

Nick had caused his own destruction through trying too hard to impress. He had become an insecure, toxic friend and partner of the worst kind. By this stage the women he attracted were all insecure and immature, only interested in superficial relationships, overly impressed by the glamour of club culture, their main concerns which clubs they could get guest-listed into. Therefore the relationships all descended into a mass of paranoia, full of age-inappropriate behaviour that ultimately only resulted in traumatic endings.

The sad truth is that Nick ended up addicted to coke and then crack, as his partying lifestyle spiralled more and more out of control. He even ended up beating up some of the women he became involved with. Basically, he lost all respect for them and for himself. Sadly he was incapable of looking at his behaviour in any depth and refused to think about his actions in any real sense. Therapy was, for him, a way of justifying his actions. He was effectively telling himself: 'I'm not that bad, at least I am trying to get help.'

As I said before, turning up to therapy or buying this book and leaving it on the shelf won't help anyone. You have to engage with your issues, otherwise, like Nick, they will just get worse. Never better. Nick eventually left therapy with me as he felt I could not help him. I believe he is now on his third therapist, and is still totally resistant to looking at his behaviour or communicating honestly with himself or others.

Nick is representative of the worst type of unfaithful relationship. This kind of serial cheating can only be resolved through lots of hard work on yourself first, even before you tackle your relationship.

ARE YOU AN INSECURITY ADDICT?

Take a look at the statements below. If you agree with four out of five of the statements you need to address as a couple the pathologically unfaithful behaviour in your relationship. Remember the emphasis on honest communication and tell each other what is happening behind the scenes of your relationship.

When you suspect your partner is the unfaithful one:

- You know when your partner goes out with their friends they will try to meet women or men.

- You think any man or woman who has the chance to be unfaithful, will be. Your justification is that 'at least it "proves" your partner is attractive ...'

- You tell yourself you don't mind what they do when you are not around as long as they are good to you.

- You don't want to discuss the unhealthy aspects of your relationship in case your partner leaves.

- You tell yourself their unfaithfulness is something they will grow out of.

Other Trust Breakers:

- You worry that every time they go out they will spend all of your money on an addiction – whether it is gambling, drugs, buying expensive champagne to show off, whatever.

- You go through the bank statements each month on the look-out for massive cash withdrawals they may have taken to feed a habit with.

- You need to check they haven't taken out loans or re-mortgaged the house without telling you.

- You keep having dreadful fantasies that the bailiffs will turn up.

- You worry that your partner will lose their job as a result of their unreliable lifestyle.

- In short, you feel it is just a question of time before they massively let you down.

If you agree with any of the above statements then you are putting yourself a firm second in your relationship. You are not valuing yourself enough to have a trustworthy relationship. If you agree with three or more then you definitely need to ask yourself, 'Why am I so addicted to being insecure in my relationship?'

The Damaging Impact of Insecurity

This type of relationship is never going to give you confidence that you are loved and valued. Therefore you will carry on living your daily life feeling unsure of your own worth, both in your relationship and everything else you do. It is a sad fact that *however we feel in our relationships tends to generalize into the rest of our life*. This is why it is so important to have a happy, healthy adult relationship, because that relationship will basically sum up how we will feel in the rest of our life.

So if you are continually choosing partners that let you down, such as Nick, you need to reflect on what is in it for you.

So What's In It For You?

- Do you feel so bad about yourself that it feels perversely good to gather evidence that you are indeed unworthy?

- Are you so desperate not to want to think about how you will progress in your professional or family life, that having a destructive but all-consuming relationship is a welcome distraction?

- Was this the pattern of your parents' relationships, so you tell yourself there is no other option, thereby basically conning yourself?

Why Don't You Like Yourself?

There is no way you just choose pathologically unfaithful partners by chance, so don't try and pretend to yourself you do. If this is a situation you keep finding yourself in, ask yourself this basic question: 'Why don't I like myself?' End your destructive relationship and work on yourself for a while, until you stop being unconsciously attracted to the cheating kind.

To establish whether you don't like yourself make two lists. In the first describe yourself in five words – your 'actual self'. Then make a list of what you would like to be – your 'ideal self'.

For example:

Actual self: Lazy, overweight, boring, unattractive, kind.

Ideal self: Vibrant, attractive, interesting, funny, kind.

The interesting and desperately sad thing about the woman who wrote these examples is that she wasn't actually any of the first things. In reality she was much closer to being the person on her ideal list, but she just could not see it because she did not like herself. This is where the trap lies – how can you see that you are being self-destructive and don't like yourself, if you dislike yourself so much that you cannot see you are being hard on yourself?

Be Fair to Yourself

One way is to imagine you are a friend of yours and ask yourself how you would describe that friend if you were talking about them. The basis of this is that people who don't like themselves are often much kinder, and in fact fairer, on their friends. So imagine you are your own friend and then see if your 'actual list' is really as bad as you first wrote. This should help you see how unfair you are on yourself, and then it is not such a leap to realize that if you are unfair on yourself in your judgements, you will also be unfair on yourself in your relationships. So you end up choosing someone who will make you feel bad about yourself, which only goes to perpetuate the myth that you are not a good person who deserves happiness.

Obviously, not all infidelity is this hopeless or pathologically destructive.

Case Study | Jenny

Jenny loved her boyfriend very much but found the desire for unfamiliar touch all too enticing. About once a year she would cheat on him. For her it was not because she did not love him, she just found new people exciting and the thrill was a type of fix she had become addicted too. However, like all addictions, ultimately it became destructive when she realized she was hurting her lovely boyfriend and emasculating him. She saw him as lovely, but not as much of a man as the men she was cheating on him with. What started out as separate to the relationship became destructive to it.

Somewhat predictably, Jenny ended up having an affair five years into their relationship and left her boyfriend for this other man. But after eight months it was all too apparent how much she still needed her ex-boyfriend – that he had been her rock. In a perverse way he had given her the strength to go after excitement in her life, so with his departure all of her zest for life departed too. She tried to get him back, but because he *was* a man he did not want to take her back. She had hurt him too much. Jenny became depressed and left her current partner and the story could have ended really sadly here.

However, the couple did reconcile. Jenny learnt the important lesson that a hot relationship based on truth and honesty is better than brief pockets of passion which last only hours, but whose consequences can last for months and even years. One-night stands can destroy a relationship. Her boyfriend also realized that he had contributed to her unfaithfulness by being too forgiving – he had, in a way, given her permission to cheat.

WHY TRUST IS SO IMPORTANT

If this reminds you of your relationship, either as the cheat or the apparent victim, you need to break this destructive pattern. This type of relationship is steeped in denial.

As the cheat you kid yourself that your cheating is not really damaging your relationship. But it is. You are deluding yourself if you believe otherwise. One of the key things that make relationships different from friendships is the degree of emotional and physical intimacy involved. If you give this to someone else, then you are giving away a part of your relationship and therefore rendering it weaker.

If you see yourself as the victim, then you are deluding yourself that this infidelity is being inflicted on you and you are powerless to stop it. This is also not true. You have control over your own actions and you can make it clear that this is not okay, and that there will be consequences. You must lay down the boundaries and the consequences that will happen if those boundaries are crossed, and you must stick to these. If you leave, you will give your partner a chance to appreciate how much they need you. If they don't come to this conclusion, then you are probably staying in a relationship where you will never be sufficiently appreciated, and that is not healthy for you at all.

BRINGING THE TRUST BACK INTO YOUR RELATIONSHIP

Your next task will be to talk through with your partner where things have gone wrong in your relationship. But before you do this, I'd like you both to agree to follow some ground rules that will ensure your talks don't degenerate into arguments. McKay, Davis and Fanning (1983) theorized these really effective talking rules.

⚒ GROUND RULES FOR TALKING

When you are the one talking, first try to make an **observation** that is:

- Direct
  and
- Non-blaming.

Observe

Being direct means that when you make an observation, you start in a way that doesn't cast any blame. You use terms such as, 'I feel we seem to be checking up on each other more.' This does not apportion blame, as it simply states how you feel. It is also an observation on the behaviour of you *both* – 'We seem to be checking up on each other.' It gets straight to the point and does not waste time with examples – which is the surest way for both of you to end up quibbling pointlessly for hours.

So, be direct. Start with your observation of how you feel, based on behaviour that you state is both your responsibilities. And as your partner will be following the listening rules, as discussed in the emotional contract earlier, this should be a case of a concise message clearly received.

Think

Next, you say what you think about your observation. Express this as your **thought**. Make it clear this is just your thought and you don't mistakenly see it as an absolute truth. This is also direct and non-blaming. So, to build on the above example, you could say: 'I feel we seem to be checking up on each other more and this makes me think there is less trust between us.'

You are not saying anything to make your partner become defensive. You are simply expressing what you have observed and how you feel about it, without laying blame or being closed as to the cause.

Feel

The next step is to express how this makes you **feel**, by naming an **emotion**. So, 'I feel we seem to be checking up on each other more and this makes me think there is less trust between us. This makes me sad, as I valued our trust.'

Again, the pattern is the same. This statement is direct, it is not emotionally loaded and it does not apportion blame.

Need

Finally, to your **observation, thought** and **emotion** you add what you **need**. So, 'I feel we seem to be checking up on each other more and this makes me think there is less trust between us. This makes me sad as I valued our trust, and I really need to trust you and to feel trusted.'

When this formula is listened to, following the listening rules outlined earlier, it gives you the best possible chance of communication that is effective, non-defensive, and will lead to a resolution. Although it has taken a few pages for me to explain the rules, when you follow them you should have only been talking for about one minute. Suddenly you can see how 15 minutes is a good length of time to talk. As you are being direct, you won't waste time talking in circles.

YOUR TASKS FOR BUILDING TRUST

These tasks will take 2 days.

Couple's Task

Talk, talk and talk some more. Try to thrash out between you exactly what has gone wrong in your relationship. You must both be completely honest. And in order to encourage honesty, you have to allow each other to speak without fear of retribution or anger. So keep anger in check. Aim to each take turns to talk and listen for 15 minutes.

Define what went wrong between you. Both of you need to take some responsibility, but with a ratio. So if the problem was cheating within the relationship, the person who cheated needs to take twice as much responsibility for the problem.

For example, in the case of Jenny, who cheated on her partner, she owned up to the fact she had been unfaithful and said she saw why she had done this. She explained her part and took 80 per cent of the blame. But her partner also acknowledged that, however unwittingly, he had allowed her to cheat by turning a blind eye, so he took 20 per cent of the blame. In practice, this meant Jenny had to do most of the making up and winning back of trust, but importantly it also meant that her partner had to work on not turning a blind eye to things. This was his area for working on.

Individuals' Tasks

Here are your tasks if you are doing this on your own, either as the undiscovered cheat in the relationship or simply as someone who has difficulties around the concept of trust.

Communicate honestly with yourself. Make a list of the benefits that cheating has for you on one side of the page, and on the other the consequences it may have on your relationship. For example: not being totally trustworthy, not being honest.

Then take a really good look at these consequences. Do they make a brief sexual liaison worth it?

If infidelity was not the issue, make a list of all the other issues that have caused you to struggle with trust. Once you have your list, look at these factors and ask yourself if this always has to be the case. Check that you weren't just being a bit paranoid. Ask yourself what you can do both to try to trust more, and to be more trustworthy.

DAY 4

 Couple's Task

Devise strategies for keeping this level of honesty up and for how you can stop anything like this happening again. For example, you might admit to each other if or when you are feeling sexually bored in the relationship, and decide on new ways to spice up your sex life.

Or you could promise to express your fears to each other if one of you feels the other is getting too close to a friend, and you are afraid something may happen. The other partner should listen and draw back from that friend, as your partner can sometimes see these things before you do.

Recommit to each other by talking about how much you both want to keep this relationship. Be open about what the consequences will be if trust is broken again.

Here is a final exercise to remember what trust essentially is.

One of you is blindfolded while the other leads you around the house or garden, or wherever. But be careful – the partner who is the guide has to look after their blindfolded partner well and prove they can be trustworthy. Once you have done this one way, swap around so you can both experience trusting and being trustworthy. This will trigger a cognitive memory of what trust is.

🧍 *Individual's Tasks*

Look again at your list, and honestly assess whether you have ever behaved in an untrustworthy way in the past. Then ask yourself how you would feel if your partner was doing this to you? All the small ways you are destroying or ignoring the trust can undermine a relationship before it starts.

If you are trying to heal your relationship without trust or being trustworthy, then you will fail. You need to have the trust in place first. Then security, and feeling valued, will follow.

TO SUM UP ...

By this time, you should be starting to feel more hopeful about your relationship. The clients who come into therapy with me usually feel a bit relieved at the end of these tasks – which would constitute their first few sessions – relieved that at least they have started trying to work things out. You should try not to worry too much about the outcome just yet – simply making the commitment to trying is sufficient at this point.

You should also have spent some time working out why and where the trust is missing in your relationship and followed the tasks that will encourage open communication about this.

You will have spent around two hours twenty minutes working on your problems so far. Doing this should mean that you feel hopeful rather than hopeless about this relationship. Hold on to this hopefulness and lean on it if you get a bit overwhelmed by the tasks in the next chapter. Remember how far you have come already; this will provide you with the motivation to prevent you from calling time on your relationship prematurely. It really will be worth your while – and your partner's – to finish all the processes outlined in the book. If you are doing this as an individual you should be able to see more clearly why trust was not solid in your past relationships. Once you can identify the past issues with trust you can prevent this from happening again. Once you have recognized negative patterns you are more able to prevent their repetition.

CHAPTER 5

THE ARGUMENT RUT
And How to Break Free From It

The next big issue to deal with is the argument rut. This may well be one of the most dangerous threats to your relationship, so as soon as you have built up the trust between you sufficiently, it is most important to look at and eliminate unhelpful arguments.

WHAT IS AN ARGUMENT RUT?

We all get stuck in ruts. Ruts of never making enough time for ourselves, ruts of never going to the gym, ruts of losing all interest and motivation at work, ruts in our sex lives where we never do anything but the same old routine, style ruts where we dress the same way for years – the list is endless. But equally common is the argument rut. The argument rut is where most of the interactions you have with your partner, no matter how they started, turn into arguments.

Case Study | Isabella and Paul

Isabella had spent a long time planning the perfect date with Paul. The whole evening they both tried really hard to show consideration, kindness, and respect for each other. Yet despite their best efforts, at the end of the evening they somehow got on to the topic of their finances and ended up having the same old argument they had had a million times before. Why? Because their relationship had fallen into an argument rut, and now, no matter how well-intentioned they both were, all roads seemed to lead to the same topic – in their case, money – an issue over which they always argued, yet never resolved.

WHAT THE ARGUMENT RUT REVEALS

Whichever particular argument rut you happen to be stuck in, it will define your relationship in some way. This is because your specific argument is likely to be triggered by your biggest fear. These fears could range from 'He does not love me enough' or 'She wants to control me,' to 'I am not good enough for this relationship.' When your thinking gets into this kind of rut, it will underpin all your arguments – whatever they start off being about. For instance, they could start as a discussion about when you are going to move in together, or about your social life, or attitudes to work, family and friends – but sooner or later they all come back, with dull predictability, to the underlying niggle. The sad truth is that if you have too many of these arguments you will literally force your biggest fear to come true. The argument will become a self-fulfilling prophecy.

WHEN DOES THE RUT START?

The argument rut occurs when a couple feel compelled to discuss the symptoms of their unresolved issues over and over again in an attempt to reach a solution. However, because of the very nature of arguments, all this serves to do is increase each person's resolve that they are right and the other is wrong. Then sides start to be taken, and every time the issues are discussed, the couple become more and more polarized from each other. Attitudes become more and more extreme until the relationship becomes overwhelmed by the seriousness of the issue. What could once have been easily resolved through rational discussion and compromise becomes a point almost worth destroying the relationship over, as the issue at the heart of the argument undermines the strength of the relationship and the love the couple share.

Case Study | Cyrus and Imogen

Cyrus believed Imogen felt more loyalty – and perhaps even more love – for her mother than she did for him. He began to fear this soon after their engagement, but thought the balance would shift after they were married. Soon after the wedding, Imogen's mother, who was unaware of Cyrus's fears, wanted to visit. Imogen thought this would be a nice idea as her mother could see their new house. But Cyrus took all this as evidence that his fears for him and his new wife were a reality.

Cyrus began to resent his mother-in-law's influence over Imogen and began to argue with Imogen over the smallest of points. They argued over the need for their best linen on her mother's bed when she stayed, over what she should be given for Christmas and many other minor points. Cyrus was actually doing this to test his theory about where Imogen's true allegiance really lay, but all Imogen could see was that Cyrus was being unreasonable and unwelcoming towards her mother. They began to argue about this constantly and their positions became increasingly polarized. As their constant arguments continued they began to try and score points over each other – Imogen began inviting her mother around even more, or involving her in decisions simply to annoy her husband. Cyrus failed to attend family functions and became openly hostile to his mother-in-law. He also became increasingly close to his own mother, who was drafted in to even up the now very firm sides.

Eventually, Cyrus could see no way out of the now intolerable situation without leaving his marriage. He firmly believed he would never be the number one priority in his wife's life. But if they could have seen past the arguments, if Imogen had taken the time to reassure Cyrus, and if he had really told her what his insecurities were and what he really felt, their relationship could well have survived. They may have cut through the arguments that were simply symptoms of their insecurities instead of splitting up over them.

ARE YOU STUCK IN AN ARGUMENT RUT?

Ask yourself the following questions:

- Do you actively try to avoid certain topics because you know they always result in conflict?

- Do you actively avoid certain people for fear that meeting them might cause friction, or avoid locations because of a fear that going to them will cause arguments?

- Are you having at least two arguments per week?

- Do you end up acting out of character during arguments?

- Do you experience a sense of déjà vu during your arguments?

- Do you find yourself mulling over hurtful things you have said or that were said to you during arguments, at least once during your daily activities?

If you have answered yes to three or more of the above questions you are caught in or nearing an argument rut.

WHY ARGUMENTS ARE SO DESTRUCTIVE

Arguments can be really destructive and often pointless. There is a big difference between interactions, which are constructive, and arguments. In order for an *interaction* to turn into an *argument* someone has to shout or advocate something so strongly that their manner becomes almost bullying. Each person within the couple becomes more interested in gaining compliance than in identifying core issues and then working together to resolve them. In other words, they have become more interested in attributing blame than resolving the issues.

Next time you find yourselves in an argument where your emotions are so overwhelming you want to scream, shout, and destroy either yourself, your partner or your environment, try and remember that this is because you are feeling desperate – and sometimes you can feel this to the point of being out of your own head with rage – not a good place to be in.

Everyone becomes someone else in an argument – someone they don't recognize and would be embarrassed ever to be identified with. However, this embarrassment can also push you further into the argument rut. You resent being forced – as you see it – into becoming this alien person who is screaming, shouting and even perhaps inflicting damage onto inanimate objects or – even more horrifying – yourself or your partner.

At this point, I need to add the caveat that when I talk about arguments I am assuming there is purely minor damage, if that, and there is definitely no medical attention needed. If you are trapped in a situation where domestic violence is frequent or serious in any way at all, then you must seek help immediately. This trap is the worst of all and can be fatal. You cannot break this trap yourself. You must get professional help.

BREAKING OUT OF THE RUT

🔧 Create Some Space

So before you scream, shout, throw, destroy something or self-combust, stop, take five deep breaths and walk away. Say to yourself and to your partner:

'Arguing now will not help anything. Let's give each other space to cool down and come back to this.' Then walk away.

If you don't, you will not be able to make the transition back to your adult rational state (*I explain this term below*) and your interactions will descend into arguments. The only thing this will achieve is more damage to your ailing relationship and further distress to the situation and yourselves. Walking away may sound like an impossible thing to do, but if you follow the techniques outlined in this chapter, you will be confident enough to believe that by walking away now you will better be able to resolve the situation later.

This technique of creating space in the heat of the moment only works if the request for space is not used to score points or to have the last word. In order to implement effectively this preventative strategy, commit the following techniques to memory so you can draw upon them whenever you need them. They will become an important part of your Emotional Tool Kit.

Tools for Creating Space

1. First, lower your tone two octaves, as the adrenaline developed during the beginning of an argument causes your voice to get louder and the tone more attacking.

2i) Next, say 'We ...' (so as to share the responsibility and not point the finger of blame)

2ii) '... are not going to get anywhere right now, let's walk away from each other ...' (again, this encourages joint responsibility and does not mean someone walks away and the other feels abandoned)

2iii) '... and talk about this when we have both calmed down.' (This implies that the issue will not be left, but will be given the deserved rational discussion later. This also takes away a sense of urgency to resolve things there and then when you are not functioning rationally.)

The reason you have to walk away when you know your emotions will cause you to attack the situation, your partner and ultimately your self-esteem, is that human nature always becomes defensive under attack.

The following example illustrates this:

Case Study | Christina and Andrew

Christina and her boyfriend, Andrew, often argued about the way they talked to each other both at home and when socializing. Andrew often accused Christina of paying him insufficient attention, and in one instance, because he was angry with her, he called her a flirt. She resented this and shouted at him for talking to her in this way as she was not flirting. This then resulted in insults flying and both parties becoming seriously distressed.

Christina and Andrew must have had this argument in different guises at least once a fortnight. This impacted very badly on them both, because they spent much of their relationship smarting from their last distressing interaction. As the argument rut became tighter and the arguments more prevalent, each of them got increasingly frustrated and tried to force the other to concede defeat in increasingly heated and potentially violent arguments. Forcing the other in this way never works, and eventually they began to lose their once very deep and real love for each other.

DISCOVERING YOUR CORE FEARS

All of this strife could have been avoided if they had been able to communicate their *core fears* to each other. Core fears are the issues that are really bothering them, for instance, 'I am not good enough for him/her,' 'I don't deserve to be happy so I won't be' and so on. They couldn't communicate these core fears so they couldn't identify the real nature of the destructive circle they had become entrapped in.

Christina feared Andrew would leave her. She was very insecure and almost paranoid that he was in some way too good for her. Her way of dealing with this was to try to prove to Andrew how desirable she was. So when she was in company she became flirtatious with other men and attentive with the women, always putting on a great show of humour and fun. This was all done so that he would feel proud of her attractiveness to others – she wanted him to see that men were attracted to her and women thought she was a lovely friend, so he would believe she was good enough for him. Christina was not attracted to anyone else – this was all for Andrew's benefit.

However, Andrew became concerned that she was too attractive for him and that she was not sufficiently trustworthy. When he saw her behaviour in company he became more sure of his hypothesis and more convinced she was going to be unfaithful, and he got angry with her. When he got angry he almost sneered at her, which Christina took as evidence of his superiority. This, in turn, made her defensive. At heart, they both shared the same fear that the other would leave them. They had became entrapped in a vicious argument circle, therefore this fear became a self-fulfilling prophecy.

Eventually, with the help of therapy, Christina and Andrew managed to discuss their real feelings, rather than acting out their fears in various different scenarios. The listening and speaking rules of observation, thought, emotion and need, as discussed in the previous chapter, worked excellently for this couple. Christina was eventually able to say, 'We argue a lot and I think it is because I fear you leaving me, so I push you away. Perhaps you fear the same, and this makes me sad because I love you and want us to be together.'

Being this honest with each other was hard to begin with, but when they began to be less self-conscious about their true thoughts the honesty started to serve as a bridge between them.

Before we start working through the week's tools and techniques for escaping the argument trap, we have to ensure you approach this task in your rational adult ego state.

THE RATIONAL ADULT EGO STATE

What is a rational adult ego state? The term may sound a little off-putting and psychoanalytical, but the logic behind it is extremely simple. And it is a powerful way to check different types of behaviour.

The adult ego state is based on a type of therapy called transactional analysis. It was theorized by Eric Berne in 1961 but is as relevant and true today. Basically, Berne realized that every person has three ego states:

1. Parent

2. Adult

3. Child.

Each and every day we will function in one of these ego states, depending on the context or situation we are in. I am sure you can think of a time when you felt as though you acted like a spoilt child or a chastising parent. Even just thinking about this for a second you will probably have realized that your communication style will vary markedly, depending on whether you are functioning and communicating from the parent, adult, or child position.

When we are in the **parent state** we are usually being either critical or nurturing, and when we are in the **child state** we are usually rebellious or compliant. As adults, we all have the capacity to function in any of these ego states and can fluctuate almost instantaneously between them.

The **adult ego state** is the rational state and it is characterized by the following type of behaviour.

Adult Behaviour

- When we are being adult we are assertive without being aggressive.

- We take responsibility for our own part in everyday activities and interactions.

- We maintain our appropriate boundaries (*see Chapter 6*).

- We treat ourselves and others with respect, even when in a heightened emotional state.

- We are kind and protective to ourselves.

Basically, in the adult ego state or adult position we make sense of the intense feelings generated by our parent and child positions. We are able to create a balance between the needs and strong emotions of the child and the rules and mandates of the parent. Adult ego states can be compared to a human computer; they are a bit like a data-processing centre that sorts through everything that's happening to you, keeping you aware of what's going on inside and outside you.

When we are in the adult ego state we make the best decisions because we are in the best position to examine the conditions of everything. We see things rationally and because we are being rational, we are in the best position from which to communicate with our partners.

Adult Communication

You know you are functioning in this state when your voice is controlled and you have properly reflected on what you want to say. Your words are intended to fuel discussion rather than wound. In the rational adult state you speak with respect for yourself and for your partner. As a rational adult you are authentic, grounded, and you don't say callous things at which you cringe in horror the next morning. I will be looking in much more detail at the different states of adult, parent and child in Chapter 8, but this information is enough for now.

Case Study | Mia and Tom

We are now returning to Mia and Tom because they got into a very revealing rut in the third week of their therapy. They kept discussing the symptoms of their problems and not the core issues (their real underlying fears). So their argument rut went something like this:

Mia: I am so busy and I have to take care of everything to do with our house as well. You are really not bothered about helping me. *(critical parent position)*

Tom: Oh, shut up! You do not see half of what I do. Who do you think organizes all the bill payments, and do you think broadband just magically appears? *(rebellious child position)*

Mia: You make me mad because you just don't try and help with the housework and … *(critical parent)*

Tom: I make you mad? What about you and all the nagging you do? *(critical parent)*

This conversation would happen in several different guises all the time. Eventually Mia was able to apply the *observe, thought, emotion, need* rule and say to Tom:

Mia: We constantly get at each other. I think I am hard on you because I am worried you are going to leave so I am almost pushing you out of the door. I don't want you to leave as I need you and need us to feel like a team again. *(adult position)*

Tom then responded: I do get angry with you because I think you just see me for what I can do for you, how I can fit into your idea of a perfect partner, to be wheeled out at family events and provide half of a great lifestyle. I want you to see me for who I am, as I see you. I also want us to be happy. I hate arguing and I also need to be a team again. *(adult position)*

Once they had done this they could start talking as rational adults, rather than adopting the critical parent or rebellious child positions.

 TASKS TO ESCAPE THE ARGUMENT RUT

These tasks will take 8 days.

If you follow the tasks listed below in your rational adult ego state, by the end of the first week you should be out of this trap.

To do this, you need to communicate your core fears (the real issues), without pretence or denial to your partner, and listen to your partner doing the same. If you are not currently in a relationship but the above scenario is familiar to you, then you need to identify the traps you have been caught up in in the past, to prevent them from occurring again in your future.

  Couple's Task

Identify the real issues behind your arguments.

First, make a list of everything you argue about. There are some examples below, and you will no doubt have your own to add to the list. If you are doing this exercise together as a couple, do not show each other these lists, but write them down separately.

 Individuals' Task

Do the same. Make a list of everything you argued about in your last relationship, or a list of any themes that you can recognize that you usually end up arguing about when you are in a relationship.

Here are some of the most frequent argument triggers I come across in my therapy:

- Photographs or belongings of ex-partners
- The influence of friends
- Attitudes towards each other's respective families
- Ways to spend your money

- Actions when socializing

- Socializing separately

- The amount of time spent at work

- Things that happened ages ago that were allowed to fester – this is particularly problematic and needs to be avoided. If something happens that upsets you it is always best to say something at the time, calmly, not months later when they will have become totally exaggerated in your mind.

DAY 6

 Couple's and Individuals' Tasks

Now look at each item on your list and try to identify exactly what it is about each issue that really upsets you.

Example 1:
Photographs/other memorabilia of ex-partners

Ask yourself: what is it about these photographs that causes you to keep arguing?

Of course, it is not the actual photograph that upsets you; this is just a bit of paper. It is what you feel that the photograph symbolizes. We rarely argue about the real cause of things, but instead tend to get stuck arguing about related, but often misleading, issues.

Now try and access the emotion behind your thoughts. So in this instance, you could feel that having old photos around means that your partner is still in love with, or has strong feelings for, their ex. However, it could be that they just see these photos as a recorded memory. At heart, what you are upset about is that you feel insecure about the way your partner feels about you, and this is making you even more insecure. You are also likely to compare yourself to their ex. Having the photographs around makes this insecurity more raw for you.

The real problem is how you feel about the way your partner feels about you, and the photographs get embroiled in this. You end up feeling, 'If he/she really loved me he/she would throw these away.' So be honest with yourself regarding what it is about your partner's attitude to these photographs that causes you such difficulties.

Example 2:
The influence of friends

Once again, question what upsets you about your partner when they are with their friends. Again, this issue is really caused by insecurity and a lack of trust. The friends are not the problem – they cannot force your partner to behave differently. What is happening here is that you do not trust your partner sufficiently to remain the same even when they are around their friends.

If the feeling behind the arguments about friends is that your partner does not like your friends, then the issue is really that your partner does not trust you to remain true to yourself when you are with them.

Either way, trust is the issue here and will be the issue in your relationship, because it does not feel stable to one or to both of you. One of you feels the relationship is so fragile and precarious that the influence of other people could break it up. It could also be that one of you suffers with such insecurity that it would not matter what the other did to convince them all was stable – they would simply not believe it.

Example 3:
Attitudes Towards Each Other's Respective Families

Again, look at what you are arguing about. Ask yourself, what are these arguments a symptom of? What is the real, underlying cause? When families become a problem this is usually an indicator that one or the other partner does not feel accepted, valued, or prioritized within the relationship. Look closely at what upsets you about your partner's family and see if it fits into one of these categories.

Example 4:
Ways to Spend Your Money

Finances are a huge cause of arguments. But what does arguing about finances really achieve? It does not make the debt disappear. Besides, shouting at someone to spend less money rarely works; in fact the opposite is usually true. What you need to do is ask yourself what it is about money that causes you to argue. Is it the way your partner spends their money? And if so, are you taking this personally? Perhaps as a sign that they are not as committed as you are to prioritizing the plans you have for the future, or the quality of life you would like to have together as a couple.

Or is it that one of you is being too controlling and dominant, and using money as a tool to be in control of the relationship, with the result that you both get stuck in limiting and labelling roles within the relationship?

Example 5:
Actions When Socializing

If you often argue when you are out socializing, as in the example of Christina and Andrew described earlier, it can indicate real insecurity. When someone feels particularly exposed, their destructive emotions – such as excessive insecurity – will become exaggerated and arguments are more likely to happen. If alcohol is involved, then arguments will be even more childish than usual. The real reasons for the arguments will be less about whatever it is you think you are arguing about and more about your respective insecurities.

Example 6:
Socializing Separately

Again, this could be about the insecurities that exist within the relationship rather than the people and places involved.

Much of what I said above about the influence of friends is applicable here too.

Example 7:
The Amount of Time Spent at Work

Assess this one in the same way. Is it really about work or is it insecurity about each other's priorities? Much of what

I said about arguments over finances will apply here – it's usually about insecurity over how important the relationship is to you or your partner.

DAY 7

 Couple's Task

Each of you now makes a list of the *real* issues behind the causes of your arguments, taken from your reflections done on days 7 and 8. In order to do this, just write out the emotions you identified concerning how you feel about the things you argue about, as you did in the last task. Do not share this list just yet.

Individuals' Task

Make a list of the real issues behind the things that have most upset you in the past, the things you usually argued about in past relationships. In order to do this, just write out the emotions you have just identified when thinking about the things you argued about in the last task.

For couples or individuals, instead of details of arguments, this list should read as a list of *emotions*, as in the list that follows:

• Insecurity

• Feeling way down your partner's list of priorities

• Not totally trusting your partner, feeling replaceable

- Feeling mistrusted

- Paranoia stemming from your own or your partner's low self-esteem

- Feeling undervalued

- Feeling disrespected.

Take time over this list. Don't rush it, as you will miss the core issues.

There are some rules for writing this list:

- Don't start with 'You are ...', as this is attacking your partner or yourself. If you do this the interaction will become defensive and not engaging. Instead:

- Write only your feelings

- Do not apportion blame.

Once you have written your list, reflect on it. Does it ring true for you?

Now destroy your list of argument topics. This list is part of the old argument rut and has now been replaced with the real issue list.

   Couple's Tasks

With your partner, swap your lists of only the *real issues*. Read each other's list, but do not talk about them yet as this process could cause an argument if handled inappropriately.

Look at your partner's list and identify similarities between yours and theirs. Also look at the differences.

Now, try and put yourself in your partner's shoes. Think about how they have been feeling. This will help you to challenge the misconceptions about each other that have been created in your relationship.

Come up with a list of solutions for your partner's issues. My examples are generalized – yours should be specific to your own relationship.

For each issue on your partner's list formulate a solution. For example:

Insecurity:

- Use language with your partner that encourages them to feel secure. Tell your partner to tell you when they are feeling insecure, and instead of dismissing this, reassure them that there is no need to be.

Feeling way down your partners' list of priorities:

- Communicate how important they are to you and do things to show them this. For instance, send quick texts during the day – say nothing except emotions, e.g. 'I love you', 'Hope all is well' etc, not 'I love you, please pick up dry cleaning.'

Not totally trusting your partner, feeling replaceable:

- Again, communication is key. Remind you and your partner why you want to be with them.

Feeling mistrusted:

- Trust your partner to go out separately, and if you are the one going out do not abuse that trust.

Paranoia stemming from your own or your partner's low self-esteem:

- Again, reassurance is most important here.

Feeling undervalued:

- Look for things your partner does for you that you might take for granted, and make a habit of thanking them.

Feeling disrespected:

- Start to talk to them as you would to a friend that you want to keep, rather than as someone whom you just expect always to be there. Give them space, don't criticize, and remember what attracted them to you in the first place.

Once again, read your list of solutions. Reassess if your partner is going to like them and whether you are comfortable with them. Really ask yourself honestly: *are you using this list to support or to attack your partner?* You must be supportive or you will lose your partner's trust.

** Individuals' Task**

If you are doing this individually, come up with a list of solutions that you will try and implement in your next relationship that will support you to overcome your relational issues, i.e. feeling insecure.

- Do not allow yourself to look for evidence of infidelity, such as trawling through their emails.

DAY 9

 Couple's Tasks

Show each other your solutions. Do not talk about them to each other, just read them. Try and see what your partner is attempting to do for you. A lot of arguments are caused by believing the worst of each other, so remember that you are both trying to help or you would not be doing this.

Start to talk to each other about the solutions and, together, construct a definitive list of strategies that you are going to try and implement. Discuss these strategies together and only have ones you both like on the list. Avoid thinking about how they will work; just consider whether you like them in principle.

Together, agree on some rules for all communication between you from now on:

- No blaming
- Taking equal responsibility – blame attribution simply traps you in the argument rut
- Not being defensive; accepting that it takes two to cause problems in a relationship.

Individuals' Task

If you are doing this out of a relationship, make another list of what went wrong for you in your last but one relationship and try to identify similarities between your last two relationships. Then come up with a definitive list of strategies for yourself that you could see might have worked in your previous relationship.

DAY 10

 Couple's Task

Produce an action plan together that encompasses all of the above strategies and try it out for 24 hours.

 Individuals' Task

If you are doing this on your own, take the time to reflect on whether or not these strategies could have fixed any of your past relationships.

Here's an example of some rules for your action plan as a couple or individual:

- You will both put equal levels of effort into your relationship

- You will both stop blaming each other

- You will both compromise equally

- Neither of you will negatively affect the other's work,

relationships with families and friends, or appropriate freedom.

DAY 11

 Couple's Tasks

List what has changed for the better for you in the last 24 hours, and what you still need to change.

Discuss the list with your partner and recognize what you have positively changed for each other, while looking at what still needs changing.

Remember to stick to *fundamental* issues like the need to be positively regarded, rather than the symptoms, such as having arguments along the lines of 'You disregard my career in this relationship.'

 Individuals' Task

If you are doing this for yourself, then list what you are more hopeful about for your next relationship and areas that are still a concern.

DAY 12

 Couple's Task

Agree to draw up a 'relational contract' in which you both agree to the points below.

Individuals' Task

Make a promise to yourself that in your next relationship you will:

• Agree to never have more than two lines of conflictual dialogue

• Agree to say 'I feel ... (for example, 'left out of things'), rather than 'You are ... (for example, 'a rubbish partner who does not know how to treat someone properly')

• Agree to remember the *core issues* and discuss these, rather than the symptoms and details that will just propel you back to the vicious circle that is the argument rut.

Getting out of the argument rut does not mean you won't still feel the insecurities you did before, but now you will not get bogged down in arguing about symptoms rather than causes. Hopefully you will become aware of each other's issues and discuss them in a rational, adult way. This will mean you constantly address the core issues, this focus of energy on the real problems means you are far more likely to deal and resolve the main threats to your healthy relationship.

GETTING THE BALANCE RIGHT

Always remember that awareness of each other's needs does not mean you have to take responsibility for them; it just means supporting each other. If one of you is very insecure, then the other will explain why they will be late home, rather than just saying, 'I will be late.' However, they will not avoid being late as they cannot change the way they live their life to pander to your insecurities.

Likewise, they will not openly comment on the attractiveness of other people but neither will they stare at the floor for fear of you believing they are gawping at others. This is the difference between empathizing and taking responsibility. You need to empathize but it is not healthy or appropriate for them to take responsibility.

Now you have learnt how to stop arguing you have created the space needed to work on the issues in your relationship. Also, you have come up with a way of talking about these issues rationally following the *observe, thought, emotion, need* rule and the listening rules. So you can say to your partner, 'I think we still clash over ... I think this is because we are both scared of losing each other (or whatever sentiment is appropriate). This worries me as I don't want to argue. Can we talk about this rationally?'

You have also developed a strategy to address the underlying core fears you both hold. This will enable you to reassure each other in your daily interactions, rather than heighten each others' paranoia.

TO SUM UP ...

By the end of this chapter you should have identified the reasons behind your arguments, and recognized that although you may argue about lots of different things, they all come down to one or two (usually a maximum of three) core issues. The arguments over, for instance, your partner's ex-lovers are simply a symptom of insecurity. So in this chapter we have guided you through identifying these symptoms, in order that you can both talk in an adult way about your relationship's core issues. This will stop your discussions degenerating into slanging matches that solve nothing.

Over the course of one week, you will have spent just 20 minutes a day identifying the core reasons for your arguments. If you find you are taking longer than this at the tasks, then ask yourself whether you are being as productive as possible. Make sure you are following the listening and talking rules I described in the previous chapter. As long as you are, then do not worry if the tasks take you longer. But if it feels as though you are going round in circles, re-familiarize yourself with the rules of communication and try and cut down the time.

Now you should start to feel some real progress – in just one week you are doing well! We now need to build on this improvement. In the meantime, take the argument and conflict avoidance techniques discussed here as a given and fundamental rule – if not for the rest of your relationship, then at least for the rest of this book!

CHAPTER 6

SEEING YOUR PARTNER FOR WHO THEY REALLY ARE
Remembering Why You're Together

In the last chapter we addressed the cause of arguments in a relationship. I explained how arguments are usually the manifestation of core fears that are not being addressed. Instead, the symptoms that arise from these core fears are re-hashed over and over again. We worked on understanding what your core fears are, and how you can get to the heart of the matter by dealing with them in a non-aggressive, non-defensive manner. As a result, your arguments should have significantly lessened, especially if you follow the 'Time out' techniques I described to prevent the arguments getting started in the first place. So now you should be in a much healthier relational space.

However, a hangover from the argument rut is that while you were arguing you will probably have crossed over some boundaries in the way you treated your partner. I have often met couples who have said so many things to cause pain to each other that they have crucially altered their perceptions of each other.

Your relationship should be very important to you. In fact, it should be one of the most important things in the world. So you should treat your partner as one of the most important people in your world. Yet many people treat their partners as if they were one of the worst, leaving them both hurt and bewildered.

Case Study | Charles and Lorna

Charles and Lorna had been together for a long time. Unfortunately the first half of their relationship had been dogged by awful arguments where they had called each other every hurtful name under the sun, and then made up a few more. They had experienced very emotionally violent and destructive rows. But they had made a big effort to stop these when they realized what they were doing to their relationship; and the birth of their first child was another massive wake-up call. So when they came to me it was not because they argued any more, but because they still saw each other as the person with whom they had had all those arguments. It was as though those awful, destructive rows had replaced any memories of what they had first seen in each other, and overridden the reasons they had fallen in love in the first place.

Charles saw Lorna as somewhat hard, strong and difficult. He described her as being demanding, a survivor, independent, and basically as 'scary when pushed'. Of course, he also saw more positive things about her, and they enjoyed their day-to-day life, but deep down this is how he conceptualized her.

In turn, Lorna felt desperately unsupported. She felt as though she always had to be tough, and when friends of theirs protected their partners she became jealous. She vividly described an incident eighteen months earlier (as women can do) when they had been at a restaurant with another couple and the two women had both ordered the same main course. When it arrived it was awful, and her friend's partner immediately said he would send it back for her. Charles did not do this for Lorna, and instead remained silent, eating his food. When the food had been duly changed, Charles had said, 'I knew Lorna was more than capable of handling that; no-one can stand up for herself as well as she can.' Lorna was, of course, more than capable of handling the situation but that wasn't the point. She did not always want to have to do it. Sometimes she just wanted Charles to do things for her, not because she couldn't but just because she really wanted to be looked after for once.

Due to their arguments, the stronger, perhaps tougher, side of Lorna was always at the front of Charles's mind, rather than her softer more vulnerable side. Charles could not be blamed for this — he had indeed seen the tough side of her for years. Equally, Lorna could also not be blamed for the situation, as she was making efforts to change that side of her character. And anyway, they had both argued with equal venom.

My task was to help them move on from wasting time apportioning blame to each other, and try instead to enable them to develop an accurate present perception of their relationship and of each other.

SEEING YOUR PARTNER FOR WHO THEY REALLY ARE

Misconceptions about your partner can cause arguments because they can lead to confusion and hurt. It is not just arguments that cause misconceptions; they can also occur when you project too much of your personality or your expectations onto your partner. Another common cause is blaming your partner for making you feel insecure or intimidated, when in fact those insecurities are self-induced and would happen regardless of what your partner says or does.

The Difference Between Personality and Behaviour

Another tendency it is important to avoid is attributing all of your partner's behaviour to their personality. So if your partner is uncharacteristically moody, instead of seeing that they are having a bad day you 'label' them as quite a moody person. Basically, in any relationship it is important to see your partner for who they are, and equally for you to be seen for who you are.

This next point, as illustrated by the following case study, is particularly relevant if you are doing this on your own.

Case Study | Dan

Dan was always being dumped after about six months. He had had many great relationships but they had all ended around this point. His last partner had left him for being 'too demanding'. Dan reported that his partner had said, 'I just can't be with you, because however much I give you, you want more.' This was not the first time his partners had told him something like this. What really confused Dan was that this did not match his view of himself. He saw himself as giving and generous, quite the reverse of demanding. Indeed, for his ex, Dan had really gone out of his way to support him and had even helped him through a family bereavement in the early days of their relationship. This turned out to be the crux of the problem.

Dan was not being excessively demanding, but he wanted to receive the same support back as he gave. As he was so considerate and kind, his partners' efforts at returning this consideration never really matched up. What Dan needed to do was to present himself to his partners in a way that was truer to who he was. Dan needed to say he sometimes had a tendency to do more for people than they really expected, and if they ever felt he was doing too much they should inform him. This way he could take the pressure off himself, and it would also take away the pressure he put them under to reciprocate in kind. Moreover, he stopped being the one who was always giving, his partners would have more space to do things for him. So Dan could sometimes be the one feeling special, rather than the one making the other feel special.

Think About How You 'Promote' Yourself

It is important to think about how you 'PR' yourself in a relationship. For example, are you doing or saying something that gives out the wrong message? Furthermore, everyone has many different sides to them. If we were all simple creatures this book would be a lot shorter than it is. So if you do have a certain side that is definitely a part of you, but not an all-encompassing or an all-defining one, make sure you try to project a balanced view of yourself so you are not seen as far more demanding, for example, or pessimistic than you actually are.

Case Study | John and Sorrell

John felt frustrated with his wife Sorrell due to her somewhat aggressive style towards the world. It was true that Sorrell had a pessimistic view of life. She thought people would let her down, or were out 'only for themselves' until they proved otherwise. But nevertheless, she did love John and think highly of him. Unfortunately for their relationship, the way in which she interacted with others touched a raw nerve with John, and fed his insecurity that Sorrell did not really respect him. John was a very considerate communicator and he felt that Sorrell's failure to be equally considerate was an indication that she didn't feel respect for him, rather than simply being a matter of her communication style.

John needed to be able to trust Sorrell and recognize her aggressive turn of phrase as just that – a turn of phrase. But he could not be rational enough about his insecurity to trust Sorrell. Further, neither did he seem to have sufficient positive regard for her that he could ignore the language she used and see beyond it to her actions.

Meanwhile, Sorrel was becoming increasingly frustrated with what she felt were John's overreactions to her conversations. It got to the point where she felt she was not even allowed an opinion. Sorrell found it almost impossible to believe that John was reacting negatively to how she put things, rather than to the content of what she was saying. In other words, her opinion would have been welcomed if it were put a little differently. Moreover, whenever John overreacted, Sorrel could not just ignore it and say to herself, 'This is his own insecurities speaking. I'll ignore his outburst and he will calm down soon.' They were not able to draw on their high regard for each other to counteract the negative vibes they were receiving from each other in their interactions.

TASKS TO HELP YOU TO SEE EACH OTHER PROPERLY

These tasks will take 1 day.

If you feel that a lot of your arguments are caused by thinking the worst of each other, follow these tasks. Once again, they are pen-and-paper-based to encourage you to construct more positive thoughts about yourself and your partner. You can do this in **one day**. If you are doing this on your own, read through the Couple's Task first and then do the Individuals' Task listed beneath it. The principles are exactly the same.

DAY 13

 Couple's Task

Today we are going to **remember why you're in this relationship in the first place**. This is important because it is the very foundation of your relationship. Now you have stopped arguing you should have cleared enough head space to remember the good times. If you can remember the good times you can bring them back. If you feel you never had good times, you can remember the potential you saw in each other in order to create a great relationship.

1. Make a list of why you think your partner fell in love with you (*List 1*). Remember – people fall in love because of positive characteristics.

   For example: Fun, attractive, full of life, energetic, caring, happy, spontaneous.

   Check your list is positive and not fed by your insecurity. If you're in doubt, ask someone you know and trust who likes you for their view of the list. Is it sufficiently positive?

2. Next make a list of the personality traits that your partner has that caused you to fall for them (*List 2*).

   For example: Caring, attractive, responsible, fun, energetic, planned, thoughtful.

   Look at each other's lists. Do you both agree with what you've each written for the first one, List 1? Do you both have an accurate perception of why you originally fell in love?

The danger is that our perceptions of each other can mutate when we have had too many arguments.

So: Fun, attractive, full of life, energetic, caring, happy, spontaneous …

can become

Irresponsible, attractive, naïve, exhausting, caring, overly optimistic, chaotic.

And: Caring, attractive, responsible, fun, energetic, planned, thoughtful …

can become

Caring, attractive, boring, potential for fun, exhausting, too cautious, overly pessimistic.

3. **Then** construct a list (*List 3*) that you both agree on as to why your partner fell for you. Check it includes items from your positive list and does not include any co-constructed negativity. List why you think they fell for you, and why you fell for them (*List 4*), and also write down things from their list of why they think you fell for them and why they fell for you.

For example: Fun, attractive, full of life, energetic, caring, happy, spontaneous.

4. **Now**, construct a list (*Lists 5 and 6*) for your partner that you both agree on, as to why you fell for them. Check it includes items from their *List 1* and your *List 2*. Check it includes items from your list on why you think they fell for you and why you fell for them, as well as items from their list of why they think you fell for them and why they fell for you (*Lists 4 and 5*).

   For example: Caring, attractive, responsible, fun, energetic, planned, thoughtful.

5. **Finally**, make sure you both have copies of *Lists 5* and *6*. Keep them somewhere easily accessible so that whenever you feel that your partner does not think highly of you, you can refer to it and see that they do. This will help you not take on their issues in such a personal way when you are interacting with them.

When doing these tasks, sometimes we can be a bit insensitive. To help avoid this I'm giving you some pointers that will be useful in any situations:

⚒ RULES TO AVOID BEING INSENSITIVE

i) Ask yourself what emotion you want to evoke in your partner by what you are saying. If it is remorse, shame, guilt and so forth, then you are angry with them and therefore bound to be insensitive. Instead, ask yourself what you are angry about and try to discuss that, then come back to the tasks when you are in the space to do so.

ii) Are you saying something in a very definite or black-and-white way? If so, you are suggesting there is only one way of seeing what you are about to say, and as we know by now there is never only one way of seeing or saying things. So be tentative and positive. For instance, instead of saying, 'I love you because you are always strong and never get bothered by things,' which could cause your partner to feel stressed and pressured into always taking on a strong role (rather like Mia and Tom's dialogues in the case study), say, 'I love that you are normally quite strong and it takes a lot to bother you.' This gives them space not to be labelled and shows you know them a bit more deeply. Everyone has the capacity to be the opposite of their normal self and showing that you understand this reduces the pressure on you both, within your relationship.

Also use these tasks to avoid being insensitive in your communications when you feel your partner does not deserve your trust or high regard, as you can read the lists and remind yourself that they do. If you both do this the positive regard, trust and respect will come back into your relationship and stop the arguments.

👤 Individuals' Task

1. Make a list of why you think your last partner fell in love with you. Remember – people fall in love because of positive characteristics. So think back to the beginning of the relationship. Who were you to them?

For instance: Attractive, funny, caring, thoughtful, level-headed, trusting, exciting.

2. Now think about how they came to see you at the end of your relationship. Did all the positives somehow mutate into negatives following too many arguments?

   For instance: Attractive, boring, overly controlling, cautious, pessimistic, naïve, insecure.

3. Look at your first list and remember that this is the real you. This is who you are going to be in your next relationship. The latter list was because of the arguments – nothing more – and can be discarded. Think only of the real you.

We have looked at developing a real picture of who your partner is, and how you can be sensitive when thinking about them and talking to them. We've done this so you can show respect for each other. I will now look at the importance of this.

THE IMPORTANCE OF RESPECT AND POSITIVE REGARD

Let's start with discussing respect. It is a basic human need to be well thought of. When we are toddlers we hopefully get our first sense of self-affirmation when we feel happiness from seeing pride in our mother's (or whoever is our main carer) eye when she looks at us. This is about seeing yourself as your mother (or main carer) saw you. If your mother looked at you with love and pride, you felt you were worthy of love and pride. This feeling is the first step in the process of developing self-respect. This is why it is so damaging for the individual when they don't receive this love and pride, as they will not start to develop self-respect as a child.

As adults, we can compare this process to how we feel when we see our partner's feelings towards us shining out of their eyes. No-one wants to feel badly thought of by the one they love. If they do, then it causes the same amount of hurt, resentment and ultimately ambivalence as it did when we were children, although we may have not been aware of it then. If you feel your partner sees you in such a way you are likely either to begin to act in that way, or to want to prove them wrong. But either way you will develop anger towards them for ever seeing you in a negative way that showed they did not respect you in the first place.

Case Study | Cate

Cate thought that her partner, Ally, wasted a lot of time during her working day and that it should be possible for her to get home a lot earlier than she did. She saw the fact that she worked late into the night as a sign of her disorganized nature, rather than hard work. In arguments she often told her that she and her business would never amount to anything and that she was a failure in her working life. Ally obviously felt desperately hurt by this and although she was disorganized, she also felt Cate was completely undermining her. She went on to work harder and more effectively just to prove her wrong. This did eventually make Cate proud of her but by this time she was so angry at her earlier harsh attitude and disrespect that she did not care. By this stage, she had emotionally distanced herself from her.

If we feel respected by our partner we enjoy being with them and we like who we are when we are with them. If we feel they don't respect us, we have two options. Either we stop valuing their opinion in order to enable us to ignore their disrespect and keep respecting ourselves, as in the case of Cate and Ally, or we stop respecting ourselves. We end up being wrong-footed and weaker in the relationship.

In order to illustrate this point, try the following exercise:

The Mirror Exercise

Stand in front of a mirror and tell yourself that you feel good about yourself. Illustrate this in your body language: stand tall, with your feet level and with equal weight on each foot. Put your shoulders back, look yourself in the eye and say, 'Hi, I am (insert name)'. Doing this should make you feel quite positive and powerful, quite pleased to be who you are because your body language is giving your brain the message that you are proud of yourself and respect yourself. Respect is like a psychological shield that we can use to protect ourselves from negativity and criticism.

Now put one foot behind the other and put your weight on your back foot (the body language equivalent of being wrong-footed). Slump your shoulders, put your chin down and lift your eyes to the mirror. In this stance you are subjugating yourself and giving yourself – and others, if you are talking to them – the message that you are inferior to them. Now say, 'Hi, I am …' You won't feel so proud of yourself, as you are not giving yourself the message that you respect yourself.

If you can feel the negative effect of not showing yourself respect in one simple mirror exercise, think about what it is like if you don't feel respected in a relationship. You will be constantly wrong-footing yourself and not feeling worthy.

Insecurity Is Like an Infection

When you are adopting the second stance, you feel more insecure because you are literally not giving yourself the right to meet things head-on and on an equal footing. I have deliberately manipulated this exercise to prove a point, but the chances are that you sometimes do this unwittingly in your relationship. When you give someone else your power and allow them not to respect you, you will feel insecure. Insecurity is like a psychological infection; it can literally seep into all aspects of your life. If you feel insecure in your relationship this will make you question your self-worth, not just in your relationship with your partner but in all aspects of your life – your friendships, work life, family life; indeed you can even get so insecure you don't want to go to your gym or to a bar or a restaurant when it is busy, as you've lost all your confidence.

In order to prevent this happening, carrying out the tasks in this chapter will help you maintain a more objective and positive view of yourself. It will allow you to give off the right messages to your partner, so they will really value you for who you are.

The following is an example of the importance of putting these tools to use in your everyday life.

Case Study | Richard and Julie

Richard fell in love with Julie because she was extremely warm, giving and kind, and because she was passionate about making a comfortable life for both of them. Julie also took life seriously, which Richard respected, although he wanted to help her not get so hurt when things did not go according to plan. Conversely, Julie loved Richard's spontaneity and fun; he had a sense of adventure she felt she lacked. Julie also respected Richard's laid-back attitude to life.

At first they complemented each other well – Julie kept them grounded and comfortable while Richard stopped them from becoming bored and made sure they kept a good work-life balance. Then they had a child. And Julie started to want Richard to be more of a father, while Richard wanted Julie to continue to socialize and be as carefree as before.

One evening, Richard phoned Julie to warn her he would be late home from work. However, Julie had decided to cook him a lovely meal that evening and give him some special attention. She said as much on the phone, telling him she would cook him dinner, but he told her not to worry about it. Richard stopped on his way home for a drink and a bite to eat. He thought this would save Julie the hassle of having to cook for him. Meanwhile, she sat at home with a lovely dinner getting cold, and when he got back there was the inevitable huge row …

Julie and Richard could have avoided this kind of row if they had kept these things in mind:

- Both parties needed to remember why they fell in love with each other in the first place, and to treat each other accordingly.

- Julie needed to remember Richard's tendency for spontaneity. She also needed to make sure he understood that she *would* make dinner and that she *would* worry about his meal, so he did need to hurry home.

- Richard needed to remember that when Julie said she *might* cook, she almost certainly *would* cook; and if there was any ambiguity he should have called to check before going into the pub.

Patterns like this happen every day in couples' relationships and sometimes they can cause a lot of damage.

Case Study | Mia and Tom

As we have seen, Mia felt Tom did not value her, and Tom felt he filled the role of boyfriend rather than being wanted for 'being Tom'.

This made Tom treat Mia as though she were a bit manipulative. If there were two ways to translate something she did, he would always pick the one that painted her in a more negative light. If she made an extra-special effort with dinner he would 'jokingly' (but actually semi-seriously) ask her what she was after.

This was hurtful but not totally destructive. However, things got worse when Tom began questioning Mia's friendships with her male friends. He had become so used to seeing her as manipulative that he started to stop trusting her to the point that every time she went out for drinks after work he would send her very harsh and nasty texts, demanding that she return home. Mia did not understand why her fidelity was suddenly coming under scrutiny and wrongly decided that Tom must be feeling guilty about something – that he was suspecting her of being unfaithful because he had been unfaithful himself.

This sounds like a bit of a leap – from both feeling undervalued to both becoming convinced that the other was cheating on them. But this does happen. Misconceptions can cause almost as much damage to a relationship under these circumstances as an actual affair.

THE IMPORTANCE OF AN ACCURATE PERCEPTION

Having an accurate picture of your partner in your mind – really seeing them for who they are – will enable you both to shape your mutual interactions to complement each other. You will be able to enjoy your daily lives without arguments or avoidable misunderstandings.

Working through this chapter should have reminded you why you fell in love with your partner in the first place. It has also probably helped you realize that the characteristics about them that often frustrate you were probably the very characteristics that most attracted you to them in the first place. You may have fallen in love with them for their spontaneity and then begun to resent their unreliability.

Case Study | David and Tony

David and his partner Tony had fallen for each other mainly because of an intense physical attraction, but also because David had such a sense of fun. He was always making life interesting, while Tony was the 'responsible one'. He literally stopped them from going broke and held them back from too many impromptu fantastic trips that were great fun but cost a fortune. This worked well while they were dating but when they moved in together their different personalities began to cause friction. David began to feel Tony was making them boring before their time – he felt as though he was being forced into pipe and slippers. And Tony began to really resent David's irresponsible attitude to life, accusing him of only wanting to go out or eat out at top restaurants, but never thinking about how they were going to pay for this, or pay the bills or decorate their home.

What had happened was that instead of complementing each other, so that they were both capable of being spontaneous and lively but could also both be responsible and careful, they had begun to polarize each other. Their resentment towards each other heightened, they began rebelling and becoming more extreme versions of themselves.

Deep down they actually had not changed at all; it was just the way they saw each other that had changed.

Perception can be changed back with just a little thought and with an open attitude that is willing to see the good, rather than the bad, in your partner. The techniques you have completed in this chapter will help you do just this.

TO SUM UP ...

This chapter has been about increasing empathy for your partner. I gave you some tasks to do in just one day, on the back of the work you did when you were learning to avoid arguments in the last chapter. Hopefully, this work meant that when you did the tasks in this chapter you were able to discuss your feelings, instead of arguing about them.

Use the lists you drew up in the tasks earlier, where you wrote down your partner's characteristics, to help you decide how best to treat them in any given situation. Consciously do this until it becomes second nature to you and your relationship begins to heal through accurate perceptions of each other and mutual respect. If you can keep remembering *why* you fell for your partner and remember why they love you, you can both act in a way that assumes you both deserve respect and high regard. This then becomes a virtuous circle – the more you both act as if you love and respect yourselves and each other, the more you feel respected and the more special you feel. Moreover, the more special you can make your partner feel. It's a win-win situation.

In the next chapter we take this one step further. We are now going to build on this new-found empathy you have for each other to help you identify both your own and your partner's personality style.

CHAPTER 7

UNDERSTANDING WHO *YOU* ARE
Developing Real Self-Awareness

This chapter is all about understanding your personality and the type of person your partner is, and how this affects dynamic interactions. In the last chapter we looked at how important it is to remember *why* you fell for each other in the first place, and how to make sure the arguments and stresses that occur in any long-term relationship do not disfigure the way you and your partner see each other, and/or yourselves, within the relationship. This chapter now expands on this, as I help you to identify your main personality type and that of your partner.

YOUR PERSONALITY TYPE

Personalities are, of course, extremely complicated, complex and changeable things. No-one should ever think that they are just one thing, as in, 'I am shy, and this is my main personality trait under any circumstance. And I can never be anything else but shy.' This is false. The people we are, the way we behave, our very identities, are fluid and constantly change across our lifespan. However, we all have some core traits.

Your Core Personality Type

Everyone has a *core personality type*. We can think of these as our main personality traits. Although they may alter in strength and importance, they are constantly present within us and they dictate the way they interact with themselves and with the world.

Your Core Interaction Style

These personality types affect our *interaction style*. Again, this is not to say that everyone only has one interaction style. You don't. You will change the way you communicate and behave towards others based on the person you are interacting with, the context, your mood, and what is happening around you. However, as with our core personality types, where there are some main characteristics that get stronger or weaker but never go away, so there are also *core interaction styles,* which can be best explained as the style you are most comfortable functioning in.

So how do core personality types and core interactional styles affect your relationship? The answer is hugely. Core personality traits will determine how you perceive your relationship and your own identity, how you define it and therefore how you respond to it and within it. Your core interactional style will underpin all of your communication and behaviour towards each other. Understanding your interaction style properly will open the door to fully understanding your partner's and your behavioural patterns. It will also help you identify any potentially destructive behaviour and stop it before it starts. It will also show you how to give your partner the benefit of the doubt, to understand when either of you acts strangely, and to understand and therefore prevent you irritating each other, as well as heading off other problems between you.

For example, are you someone who only 'hears' criticism and unconsciously blanks out any positive messages? Or do you always end up doing everything for everyone? Or do you expect your partner to behave more like a parent to you and therefore allow you not to take responsibility for anything? Personality styles and boundaries will obviously have a profound effect on you in your relationships. This chapter aims to give you a deeper insight into your personality type, particularly in relation to the way you interact within your relationship. It will make you more aware of your *psychological boundaries*, and how you can change these in ways which will be conducive to healthier relationships.

THE TYPICAL PERSONALITY TYPES

Our personality types define the way we interact with the world. They are a consequence of the way we feel about ourselves and our relationships. Typical personality types are:

1. The Pessimist
2. Always Under Attack
3. The Unrealistic Optimist
4. 'I'm Out for Myself'
5. 'I'm Owed Everything'

6. The Helpless Victim

7. 'Must Be Strong'

8. The Nurturer

9. The Rational Adult.

As I have already stated above, I am not suggesting that you will be able to look at this list and think, 'Yes, that one is me – just that one, and I am that one in all circumstances!' This is not the point of the exercise. Instead, I want you to look at the list and think about whether you ever adopt any of these personality types in any given situation, and if so, to what extent. In order to help with this I'll explain the characteristics of each trait.

1. The Pessimist

Basically, pessimists are defined by the tendency to think that everything will probably go wrong. This type of person envisages problems before they have even really begun. So they could be thinking about doing something, then decide, for example, 'I can't do that because it will be raining, not worth the money, too much effort, not as good as everyone says, boring, people don't really want me to go and so on ...' The pessimist always has an endless source of negative examples.

The problem for a pessimist in a relationship is that they are always expecting it to go wrong, so in a way they cause this to happen. It becomes a self-fulfilling prophecy. If you spend your time looking for potential catastrophes in your relationship, you are by default focusing on the negative. And as you know, if you think about something a lot you cause it to feel more real. Therefore, if you are constantly thinking about possible problems within your relationship, you will inevitably feel the relationship is more vulnerable than it actually is.

Case Study | Mia and Tom

Tom definitely had some pessimistic traits. (Remember, no-one will be only one character style all of the time, and we are identifying traits here, not whole people.) Tom generally felt pessimistic about life and saw a lot of negatives in his job, social life and in his relationship. In his job, he always thought he was being taken for granted. Even before he started a project he would convince himself that someone else would take the credit for it. He was not so pessimistic that he could not see that he was good at his job, but as the pessimism had to creep in somewhere he somehow decided that although he would be able to do a good job, no-one would thank him for it, or recognize his work.

In his relationship he felt Mia did not love him for who he really was. Again, he realized that she did love him and his pessimism could not take that away from him, but as in his job, it crept in when he came to evaluating that love. He negatively decided that she only loved him for what he could do for her and not because she really appreciated him.

2. Always Under Attack

If a person feels that fundamentally everyone is against them, they will adopt an 'under siege' mentality. This results in them responding to everyone in a defensive fashion, as though everyone deserves mistrust until proved otherwise. The effect this has on their boundaries is that they do not allow real happiness, trust or hope into their lives. Basically they can become too cynical, which in turn only leads to further bitterness.

This personality type is evident in aggressive drivers, or people who push onto Tubes and trains as though everyone is deliberately trying to keep them from reaching their destination. This kind of behaviour will have clear negative effects on any intimate relationships: this personality does not allow themselves to trust their partner or believe that their partner loves them for who they are. In other words, they do not believe that they are good enough to be in a relationship or deserving of happiness.

The following example illustrates the effects this personality type has on the boundaries within their relationships.

Case Study | Saffron

Saffron felt that at heart everyone was out for what they could get, and that therefore she always needed to be on her guard. Her partner had a very different attitude and Saffron became angry with him for not being sufficiently cynical. She interpreted his optimism as naivety. In the end, she felt she needed to overcompensate for his enthusiasm by being even more bitter and defensive. She would only let negative aspects into her life and ignored all the positives, basically disregarding any evidence from her life that she did not have to live as if she was always under siege.

The result was that Saffron and her partner became so polarized from each other that they could no longer live together. Instead of their different personality types complementing each other and compensating each other's shortcomings, they ended up locked in a feud about who was right and whose way of looking at the world was the more effective. Ultimately, Saffron never allowed herself to feel good about anything, or to enjoy even their social life. At the other extreme, her partner never allowed himself to express any disappointment or negativity out of determination not to concede a point to her. Saffron's whole attitude became a self-fulfilling prophecy – she made sure her relationship was itself under siege and eventually it was, predictably, defeated.

3. The Unrealistic Optimist

This personality type is the direct opposite to the one above. The unrealistic optimist believes that basically everyone is good and that they will always be treated as they themselves treat others. Although this can be seen as commendable, it has the downside that it can leave that person open to disappointment when their expectations prove to be overly high. If this disappointment is overwhelming it can then lead to bitterness. There is a fine line between being enjoyably optimistic and allowing yourself to become too vulnerable to possible mistreatment.

The appropriate way of interacting optimistically is to allow all the happiness and evidence that the world is basically enjoyable, and relationships are kind, into your boundary, while also being aware that this is not always going to be the case. When negativity does strike you can then deal with it, rather than naively denying it. Naïve denial can be seen when a partner continually forgives their partner for wrongdoings against them, with the justification that this 'last time' really will be the last time. Ultimately they end up giving their partner numerous last chances until they feel defeated, hurt, full of self-blame, and bitter. This personality type is also likely to come undone quickly if they do not give themselves adequate self-protection and make themselves a priority.

Case Study | Kay

Kay felt she loved her partner within weeks of meeting him. And within six months, she had devoted herself to him psychologically, emotionally, physically and financially – in fact, in every possible way. She felt it was a fairy-tale romance and refused to acknowledge any hint of reality in their relationship. As far as she was concerned, everything had to be perfect at all times. This unrealistic, fairy-tale outlook meant that she ignored all the times she should have implemented some firm boundaries regarding his behaviour and how she was treated within the relationship.

For example, if her partner was an hour late for dinner she told herself he must have had a good reason, and she told him there was no need to apologize. She chose to ignore it whenever he failed to thank her for doing something for him. Basically, she taught him that he did not have to respect her. This was very sad, because he started out by respecting her but ended up taking her completely for granted and hugely undervaluing her.

The relationship ended with her hugely resenting him and feeling incredibly let down, with an aggrieved sense of 'I gave him everything and he just took it without caring.' Kay had crossed the fine line between extreme hope and idealistic optimism, and bitter disappointment. Her perception of her relationship had no realistic middle ground – it started out as a fairy tale and ended as a tragedy.

4. 'I'm Out for Myself'

This personality style is as bitter as 'Under Siege' but is aggressive rather than defensive. The associated interaction style is more attacking. This person basically invades other people's boundaries and becomes overbearing. In order to justify this, they need to feel that other people in some way 'deserve' to be invaded, so they tell themselves that 'they are just looking out for myself because if I don't, no-one else will.' This results in them inhabiting a fairly bitter space because they can't allow trust and kindness into their personal boundary. If they did, it would threaten their resolve to live selfishly, without guilt. We all see this type of person in our everyday lives – they never buy their fair share of rounds at the bar or invite you back for dinner. They take without giving, and seem not to care.

This 'take all you can get' style of interacting does not make for mutually happy relationships and ultimately usually ends with the person being left numerous times by exasperated partners.

Case Study | Carise

Carise felt that she had had to work hard to achieve any success in her life and no-one was going to stand in her way. She seemed to live with the sense that people would take her success away from her if they ever had the chance, so she had to appear strong at all times. This meant she would not tolerate anything remotely tricky or challenging in her relationships. She fought hard whenever she felt remotely uncomfortable. In other words, she became exactly like the person she was always on the look-out for.

In order to protect herself, she became someone from whom others needed protection. Ironically, she worried so much about being bullied or walked all over that she ended up doing all the bullying and the walking over others herself. She was so worried her partner would boss her around that she became unbearably bossy. On one occasion, when he had wanted to attend a very close friend's party, she made him come with her to a friend of hers instead, by screaming and crying that his resistance to coming with her was not about how much he valued his friend but about how little he cared for her. She basically bullied him into submission. Eventually, in order to protect himself, her partner left her, as they all did, and the security she longed for kept evading her.

5. 'I'm Owed Everything'

We have all met people like this, people who believe they deserve to get what they want without trying at all: people who become aggressive when they do not get what they want – even if they have put little or no effort into achieving it. You may even recognize this in yourself. This is a very difficult interactional style and is not conducive to successful relationships. These people take without giving anything back, without even realizing it. They let all the ways in which they feel 'they have been hard done by' cross into their boundary so that they can feel sorry for themselves and self-indulgent, without letting what they haven't done or what others do for them, into their view of the world.

Case Study | Catrina

Catrina had a very good career and a not-so-good relationship with someone who was very similar to her, in that they were both scathing of others and liked to elevate themselves and their own self-importance. However, their relationship became stuck in a rut when they both felt it should be successful without either of them needing to work on it, or help it to progress in any way. As they were both so similar, neither could see that they were doing anything to maintain the 'stuckness' of the relationship and both were mystified as to the cause of their problems. This mystification became a vicious circle as it caused them both to feel even more defensive and critical of everything – except, of course, of themselves and their mode of interacting.

They were the type of people who turned up to meet friends and expected to be entertained. They would not make the effort with others but expected everyone else to fuss around them. They also made everything 'not their problem'. If a friend asked for a lift they would think nothing of refusing to help out. However, if they wanted something from a friend they would manage to present it in such a way that their friend was left with little choice – they either complied or they appeared rude.

How this manifested with each other was very interesting. If Catrina did something for her partner, such as pick up his dry-cleaning, she would think she had done him a huge favour. But as her partner equally expected things to be done for him, he rarely said 'Thank you.' Catrina felt he was the most selfish person in the world and never did anything for her. However, he did do things for her – for instance, he often prepared her meals. But she also did not really acknowledge this as, like him, she expected this as her due. She also hardly ever said 'Thank you,' leaving him feeling exactly as she did. They both truly believed that they were with the most selfish people in the world and that they alone were the kind and altruistic ones in the relationship.

6. The Helpless Victim

This boundary style is one of the most self-damaging. A person with this perception of themselves will only let in evidence that confirms that they are always going to be one of life's victims. They believe that they are destined to be a victim in their intimate relationship, in their friendships, with their family, and at work. The tragedy is that if you feel you are a victim you will be treated as one.

This self-fulfilling prophecy stems from the fact that because you expect to be treated like a victim, perhaps because you have been treated badly before, you will not try to prevent it by standing up for yourself. You expect to be mistreated, so you do not put up the right kind of self-protecting boundaries. This obviously can have grave consequences, the most extreme being domestic violence. (I am definitely not saying here that because people act like victims, they deserve to be treated as such. I am saying that victimization is an awful, vicious circle to get trapped in.)

But acting like a victim also happens to most people on a much smaller scale, on an everyday basis. If you are waiting to pay for something in a shop and expect that someone will ignore you, or push in front of you, then when they do you don't say, 'Excuse me, I was next.' You let it happen. Then, because it has happened once, you are almost resigned to the fact it will happen again the next time you shop.

Tragically, those who have victim personas invariably end up feeling so disempowered they can no longer make decisions, so they end up having to abdicate responsibility, which only serves to increase their sense of victimization. The victim persona believes that they will always be abused – by their lives, their partners and/or their employers, by bad luck, by life in general, in fact. And they also believe there is nothing they can do about it. In other words, they have learnt to be helpless.

This boundary style, or rather lack of one, is the most dangerous of all because the person's 'protective voice', or drive to protect themselves, has been all but eliminated, leaving them open to the most destructive and dangerous relationships.

The Importance of the Protective Voice

Our 'protective voice' is the reassurance we give ourselves that we deserve 'better' when things are going badly. It is what enables us to be kind to ourselves. Your protective voice is what allows you to tell yourself you need the day off work when you are ill, or that you can have that extra hour in bed when you really need the rest. In our relationships, our protective voice is the one that tells us not to rush so much in order to do an errand for our partner, that we can do it tomorrow if we can't fit it in today. Your protective voice is also where you get the reassurance that you are too tired to cook for you both tonight and that it is okay to just get a take-out. Your protective voice is also useful when you say, 'Enough is enough.' It is there when you need to say you will not put up with whatever your partner is doing that is upsetting you any longer, and that they need to change their behaviour. Your protective voice allows you to tell them that.

Although this protective voice will be weakest in anyone who has a tendency to fall into 'helpless victim' mode, it is well worth being aware of no matter what your personality type.

STRENGTHENING YOUR PROTECTIVE VOICE

If you haven't listened to your protective voice for a long time it will be quieter than is healthy. So let's work on bringing it out, by looking at a few examples of the mistaken assumptions that we can make when our protective voice is not loud enough. And here are some of the replies we should make.

Mistaken Assumption 1: *It is selfish to put my needs before the needs of others.*

Protective Voice Reply 1: **Of course you have a right to put yourself first, at least as much as you put others first.**

Mistaken Assumption 2: *It is shameful to make mistakes; I need to be perfect.*

Protective Voice Reply 2: **Why do you expect perfection from yourself and not others? You and everyone else have the right to make mistakes.**

Mistaken Assumption 3: *If I can't get others to understand my feelings, then my feelings must be wrong.*

Protective Voice Reply 3: **You have the right to be your own judge and to accept and validate your own feelings.**

Mistaken Assumption 4: *I should respect the views of others more, as they probably deserve more power. Keep my differences of opinion to myself. Listen and learn.*

Protective Voice 4: **You deserve to give yourself power and have a right to your own opinions and convictions.**

Mistaken Assumption 5: *I should be flexible and not expect too much. Others have good reasons for their actions and it is not polite to question them.*

Protective Voice 5: **You have a right to protest about any treatment or criticism that feels bad to you.**

Mistaken Assumption 6: *Things could get worse, so don't try and change things.*

Protective Voice 6: **You have the right to have your life as close to ideal as you can get it. As long as you are not causing others harm, then of course you can try and get things more your way.**

(Adapted from *Messages: The Communication Skills Book* by McKay, Davis and Fanning 1983. Oakland, CA: New Harbinger Publications)

Case Study | Vera

Vera spent all of her time caring for others. Although she knew she was being put upon, she told herself she did not deserve any better. Her protective voice had been effectively silenced by years of putting up with a selfish husband. Vera made excuses for him, such as, 'He always comes home late from the pub in the summer because he does not realize the time. When he looks outside the window, it's still light, even at nearly 10pm, and that's why he is always so late for his dinner.'

Vera never thought about what she wanted. When she came to therapy with me, we started by working on getting her to think about this, starting with very small things, such as what she wanted to eat or to wear. We started off with these because Vera couldn't claim these decisions were unfair on others, and therefore couldn't discount them. So we started with things that only affected her and then moved on to what she wanted to do with her time. After a few months Vera began to get used to asking herself what she wanted from normal, everyday situations, and her protective voice began to speak to her again unconsciously. Her own preference for things started to pop into her head without her consciously having to ask herself, 'What do I want?'

Eventually, Vera was able to apply this to the way others treated her. She began to ask herself, 'What do I want from this interaction or even this relationship?' She began to stand up for herself by voicing her preferences and expectations to her partner. Her protective voice enabled her to tell him that if she made him dinner for 8pm she wanted him home then to eat it. It sounds a small step, but for Vera it was monumental.

7. 'Must Be Strong'

This personality style is almost the direct opposite to that of the victim personality. People who feel they have to 'be strong' try never to admit their vulnerabilities or insecurities, even to themselves. They never allow themselves to seek help and often end up making life needlessly hard for themselves. They believe weakness is a fault and unacceptable in them, even though they accept it in others. The personal boundaries they build up as a result of this mean that they only allow in evidence from their daily lives that it is not acceptable for them to be weak, and that therefore they have to pretend they are psychologically indestructible. This often leads to feelings of loneliness and a sense of being overwhelmed. But of course they are never really able to acknowledge these feelings, until it is almost too late and they are really struggling to cope.

The 'be strong' persona also sometimes has a tendency to create challenging situations for themselves deliberately, so that they have a chance to prove how good they are under crisis.

Case Study | William

William and his family were attending a wedding that started at three in the afternoon. In order to be there on time to have a coffee, and not to have to rush ridiculously, they needed to leave at twelve. At midday, William's children and partner were ready to go and all went looking for him so that they could depart. It was at this time William decided to get in the shower. He finally emerged at 1pm, ready to go. He got into the car in a leisurely fashion and when everyone expressed their concern at being late he shouted at them not to panic, he would get them there. He then drove like a madman and the journey was very fraught. They arrived with literally seconds to spare. On arrival, William congratulated himself on being strong and on not panicking like everyone else and managing them to get there on time. He was very pleased with himself for averting the crisis when in fact he had caused it in the first place.

Case Study | Jane

Jane tried to be strong for herself, her children, and her partner. In fact, she spent so much time ignoring her own needs and never admitting she needed support, that her partner understandably took it for granted that she would always be okay. He almost forgot that she might have needs and insecurities, just like everyone else. But when her children left home, Jane lost her sense of purpose. Without her children to be strong for, and without any adversities to be overcome, she felt lost. But when she tried to communicate her feelings of loneliness to her husband, she was devastated to find that he had forgotten how to support her.

8. The Nurturer

This type of person is rather like a nurturing parent. They are the type who cares for everyone and everything, often with the exception of themselves. The degree to which you care for yourself depends on how much self-esteem and sense of self-worth you have. The nurturing parent persona will often do everything in their relationship without expecting anything back in return. Indeed, when they do get something back, it is often because they have facilitated their partner to be kind to them. The nurturer gets satisfaction from helping others to such an extent that they have almost forgotten that they can gain satisfaction from other sources as well, like doing nice things for themselves.

The problem with being a nurturer is that at some point you invariably cross the line into martyrdom. Perhaps you do so much for other people, things they never asked you to, that they begin to resent you, as it gives them no space to do any nice things for you. Furthermore, if you focus so much on others and not yourself it can cause those close to you to feel guilty about how much you sacrifice yourself for them – unless they are completely selfish and the type to expect everything.

Case Study | Jack

Jack did everything for his boyfriend. He saw this as his way of supporting someone he perceived as troubled. However, his boyfriend Doug interpreted this support as evidence that Jack was desperate to cling on to him, and this inflated his ego and made him respect Jack less. Ironically, he began to perceive Jack as being needy, rather than supportive.

Jack planned his own birthday. He invited his friends around and he planned what he was going to cook – his favourite meal for his birthday supper. Not only did his partner not offer to help, but he asked Jack to change the menu to that of his own favourite supper. So on Jack's birthday, Jack cooked what Doug wanted. It got worse. Jack told Doug what he wanted for his birthday and Doug just gave Jack the money to buy it. (They both had high-powered jobs and neither had more free time than the other.) So Jack went out and bought his own present, a beautiful watch. When their friends admired it, Jack proudly told them Doug gave it to him for his birthday.

Jack had actually convinced himself that Doug was being kind enough to him on his birthday, despite the fact that he had made no effort at all. Sadly, Jack could not look after himself. He focused solely on attending to others.

9. The Rational Adult

This is the personality type we should ideally all be striving for most of the time. I will be looking at it in much more detail in the next chapter. The Rational Adult is someone who truly has insight into their core personality, and who can accept themselves for who they are, while working on their insecurities. This person can let both the positive and the negative into their boundaries, but knows how to reject the damaging aspects, or those that are truly beyond their control. They take appropriate responsibility for themselves but do not seek to take responsibility for others, although they will be supportive where necessary.

The Rational Adult assertively communicates their needs and boundaries but they are neither passive nor aggressive. They seek to be grounded in reality rather than in denial or fantasy. They can have fun and be serious in equal measure, and they can work on their relationship while also attending to their own needs. In other words, they have a healthy balance – a healthy approach to themselves and their relationships. Moreover, because they are like this, they encourage their partner to behave in the same way too, as rationality and healthy relationships are exactly the opposite of the vicious circle syndrome – they are a virtuous circle.

Rather than give you an example, in the next chapter I am going to show you how you can start acting like a rational adult, if you don't always already! Eventually, if you continue to act like a rational adult in your relationships you will start to think and then feel like one, in a very virtuous and positive pattern.

🔧 YOUR TASKS FOR DEVELOPING SELF-AWARENESS

🕐 These tasks will take 4 days.

DAY 14

👥 *Couple's Task*

If you are doing this with a partner, first you should both quickly read again the golden rules of communication (*the Listening Rules as set out in Chapter 3, and the Talking Rules as set out in Chapter 4*), as clear and open discussion is key to the next few tasks.

Once you have recapped these talking and listening rules, take a piece of paper and draw a circle on it. In the middle of the circle write a list of things under the heading, 'What I take responsibility for'. On the outside of the circle write, 'What is beyond my control'. Then fill it in.

So within the first circle you write down the things you currently take responsibility for. For example:

My career being the best it possibly can be

Our debts

Our house – keeping it clean

My partner's career

Social life – making sure we keep our friends

Making sure partner sees his friends

My family – making sure we see them and I am a good daughter

His family – make sure he does not lose touch with them

Repairing his relationship with his brother

Partner's mother's moods – trying to smooth them over

My friends' happiness – supporting them through hard relationships

Partner's moods

Making sure my partner has enough time to dedicate to his hobbies.

Then outside the circle you write down the things you don't take responsibility for. For example:

My fitness

Paying bills

Our car.

It is important that this first list describes your life *as it is now*. Note down what you accept responsibility for in your life and what you reject, as you are *now*. This will help you to see what you take as your responsibility and what you don't. Listing it down in front of you will enable you to see whether you only take responsibility for things you can realistically control, or if you unnecessarily give yourself a hard time trying to be all things to all people.

From our example above, we can see that the person who wrote this list is taking far too much responsibility for those around her. She is taking on all the responsibility for all the couple's relationships – even for her partner's family and friends. She is not asking him to share the responsibility of their house, and she is even taking on the stress of both their careers. She is spreading herself dangerously thin.

Her lists show signs of the 'be strong', 'nurturer', and even the 'idealistic optimist' personality types, because she is forcing herself to try too hard at life and to feel responsible for things that are, quite frankly, not her responsibility. However, she is not taking responsibility for her own fitness because she is putting herself second to the happiness of those around her. This is the behaviour of a martyr and it is not conducive to long-term happiness. As things stand right now, her partner only has to take care of the bills and the car – nowhere near enough for a healthy, balanced relationship – and eventually she will resent all the effort she makes, even though she has allowed him to take her for granted.

▮ *Individuals' Task*

Think of how you usually act in your relationships, and how you act in your life as it is now, and follow the next task.

DAY 15

 Couple's and Individuals' Task

List everything you take responsibility for within the circle, and try to devise a strategy for how you can work towards taking responsibility for each item. For example:

Things I take responsibility for	Strategy
My career being the best possible	Work within realistic realms as best as I can
	Explore other possibilities. Keep knowledge up to date
Our debts	Pay off all our debts (but this sounds unfair as it is a shared item, so strategy should change to pay off half the debts)
Our house – keeping it clean	Clean all the time (but again, as shared item should share half the responsibility)
Partner's career	Cannot take responsibility for partner's career so no strategy – can just be a listening ear
Social life – making sure we keep our friends	Social life – can't do it all. Need friends to return invites so don't put too much pressure on self
Making sure partner sees his friends	Can't take responsibility for his friendships, other than trying to make sure he doesn't stop seeing his friends completely

My family – making sure we see them and I am a good daughter	Can only be good enough daughter – can't put so much pressure on self
His family – make sure he does not lose touch with them	Need to let partner take responsibility for his own family as they are his family
Repairing his relationship with his brother	
Partner's mother's moods – trying to smooth them over	
My friends' happiness – supporting them through hard relationships	Can't care for everyone, can't be perfect friend as not possible
Partner's moods	Partner has to regulate his moods, as I do mine
Making sure my partner has enough time to dedicate to hobbies	Partner has to look after his own hobbies

If you find it difficult to come up with a strategy to help any situation, it is probably because it is something you should not really be taking responsibility for in the first place. It will most likely be an example of something you should accept is simply not your issue. In which case it is time to stop feeling guilty about not being able to influence it. Your personality type will heavily influence how much you take responsibility for. If you are someone who has strong tendencies to the victim, optimist, or nurturer personalities, you will be trying to do too much. This task will help you balance it out.

DAY 16

👥 👤 *Couple's and Individuals' Task*

Now make a list of everything you put outside the circle – that is, all the things that you wrote were beyond your control. This task will check whether you are taking enough responsibility. If you have traits of the 'I'm owed everything' or the 'pessimist', you will probably not be taking enough responsibility. So, next to all the things you think are beyond your control, see if there actually is a way you could effectively manage them. For example:

Beyond my control   **Strategy**
My fitness
Paying bills
Our car

You actually can have a strategy for taking responsibility for your fitness. You can go to the gym, or do other exercise, and watch your diet. So you should move this item to within the circle.

Responsibility for paying the bills could be shared with your partner, as could maintaining the car.

This should help you see how you can balance things out. If you tend to take more than you give, you will see how you and your relationships could benefit from you doing more.

DAY 17

👥 👤 *Couple's and Individuals' Task*

Write new lists based on what you have learnt from these tasks. The aim is to have a much more realistic and less pressurized view of your responsibilities in life, and what you can do for your relationship.

So a new list of what you now take responsibility for could look like this:

My happiness

My career being the best possible

Halving our debts

Our house – doing half the chores

Partner's career – being supportive

Social life – making sure we invite friends and return invites as far as possible

Doing enough to see family

Being supportive to others when possible

My fitness

Sharing responsibility for car and bills.

A new list of what you can't take responsibility for could look like this:

Making sure partner sees his friends

His family – making sure he does not lose touch with them

Repairing his relationship with his brother

Partner's mother's moods – trying to smooth them over

My friends' happiness – supporting them through hard relationships all of the time

Partner's moods

Making sure partner has enough time to dedicate to his hobbies.

TO SUM UP ...

Now you have worked through this chapter you will have a clearer understanding of your personality type and how this affects the way you relate with others. You should also understand how this interacts with your partner's personality type and the way they relate to others too.

While working through the tasks, you should have taken four days at just 20 minutes a day to increase your own self-awareness and your understanding about your partner.

You will know if you have really succeeded in doing this if you can now see how you both contribute to your relationship's problems. Greater understanding of yourself and your actions, as well as your partner and their actions, will help you to eliminate the culture of blame. You should now realize that it really does take two to tango and it will never be just one of you who deserves all the blame for any dysfunction within your relationship.

CHAPTER 8

BEHAVING LIKE AN ADULT
The Key to Healthy Relationships

This chapter is all about gaining emotional maturity in your relationships. Within relationships emotional maturity is as important as love and respect. It means you are able to act sensibly in challenging situations, that you have the skills to negotiate the difficult times and can even prevent them from escalating into really rocky patches. Everything in this chapter builds on all of the previous work you have done, and will help you to consolidate it. You are always working towards the ultimate aim of being able to function as a rational adult in your relationship.

Adult functioning is based on giving both yourself and your partner respect and space within the relationship. It is about recognizing that being in a relationship is about sharing time together, rather than owning each other. Relationships are not about ownership. Being emotionally mature and rationally adult enables you to communicate properly with your partner. It also allows you:

- to follow the golden rules of communication (*these are so important that I recommend you read them again quickly now – see pages 34 and 58–60*)

- to recognize that your partner can and should be your best friend

- to realize that you need to build your partner up and make them feel important

- not to overreact when you have problematic times. Don't catastrophize and think everything is ruined. Instead, stay calm and try and reduce the stress in any difficult situation, instead of adding to it.

The rational adult stance is also crucial for getting out of the argument rut, as you need to be talking like an adult, and yes, following those communication rules again, to minimize the chance of an argument coming from nowhere. As we discussed in the last chapter, the rational adult personality style is the one most conducive to a happy, healthy relationship.

No-one can be completely rational all of the time. So don't give yourself too hard a time when you do something that gives your relationship a bit of a hammering. Just try and make sure it is as brief a beating as possible before you collect yourself together once more. As I stated in the introduction, no-one can have a perfect relationship all of the time, nor can you expect always to be happy with it.

There's a lot of truth in the saying that life isn't always a bed of roses. But whenever the relationship or your interactions go sour, and the arguments and tears return, if you can remember the work you have done in this book, you can pull the relationship back together again and turn the arguments into proper discussions. Furthermore, you will remember how to stay within the boundaries of common decency and respect for your partner, rather than shooting from the hip in a futile attempt to wound. You will have the maturity to recognize that ultimately the person who gets the most hurt will be you, if you breach the trust you have spent so much hard work in gaining.

WHAT BEING AN 'ADULT' MEANS

Being an 'adult' does not mean being dull or boring. You don't have to be aiming for a 'pipe and slippers' relationship (unless you want to!). You are aiming to behave like two people who can recognize their needs within the relationship and meet them in whatever state is required: fun, serious, calm, excited, whatever. Being adult means you can be whatever you want to be, as this will help you stay rational and grounded in whichever state you are functioning. However, the barriers to being an adult in your relationship are the other two ego states, parent and child.

Let's just look at where you are at in your relationship right now:

Are You a Parent Figure?

Do you find yourself often doing things that you do not really want to do? Have you ever:

- been watching television with your partner after dinner and found yourself making them a sandwich because they are still hungry?

- found yourself driving for the fourth Saturday in a row because your partner wants to drink?

- found yourself cancelling your plans so that you can be there when your partner calls, or even stayed at home despite having plans in case they turn up?

- paying for the holiday/weekend away again?

- feeling grateful that they like you enough to have sex with you?

If you have answered yes to three or more of these, you are still functioning in a nurturing parent mode. You feel compelled to care for all your partner's needs so that they won't leave you. Basically, you cannot believe that you are sufficient as you are, so you are almost trying to compensate for being you.

Now, a bit of nurturing is a good thing. We all want partners who can bring us tea and toast when we feel sick or even help us nurse a hangover. But we also want to be the type of person who is capable of caring and supporting. We just don't want to have to be like this all the time. We all need to be able to care for ourselves, to wrap up when it is cold, to eat healthily, to stay in if we are too tired to venture out, to support ourselves through the next promotion and generally be able to know when we need to make ourselves and our wellbeing our own top priority. So a bit of nurturing parent for others and towards yourself is healthy. But when you spend your days caring for others, and not yourself, without getting anything back, you know it is time to change.

THE DIFFERENCE BETWEEN NURTURING AND PARENTING

This chapter is not for a moment advocating banishing all the nurturing aspects of your relationship – what a cold and pointless relationship that would make. But it is about making sure you nurture your partner only when necessary, and that you make sure you receive that nurture back in equal measure. It is also about making sure you nurture yourself as much as you do others. We also have to make sure we nurture, rather than parent. Providing nurture means providing care and support. Behaving like a parent towards another adult means you are being over-restrictive and over-protective.

Case Study | Mia and Tom

Mia thought that Tom needed her to be interested in what had happened during his day and in his career. And he did – after all, everyone wants their partner to show an interest in them. However, whenever Tom started talking about things that had happened that day, Mia would invariably jump in with her view on how he should have handled his day, often interrupting his descriptions to tell him what she would have done in that particular situation. Listening to your partner and showing them support is nurture, but saying, 'Oh, I would have done …, honey,' is parenting. Nurture shows love. Parenting also shows love but feels far more restrictive.

Here is another example of this difference. Once when Tom was ill, Mia was wonderfully caring. Like many men, he had 'man flu' and was convinced he was dying. He needed her to look after him all weekend and she indulged this because she recognized that everyone needs to feel a little cared-for when they are ill, and that adults can feel like children when sickness strikes. However, a few days later, when Tom was recovering, Mia literally forbade him to return to work, which caused him a huge amount of stress over a missed presentation. The very same care that had been nurturing and supportive a few days earlier became inappropriately parental three days later.

The rule of thumb is to ask yourself how you feel when you are offering the support. Do you feel kind and caring, or forced into 'acting like his mother'? If you ever start to feel like your partner's mother – or father – stop. Stop taking responsibility for things that are probably not in your control. Stop trying to be a nurturing parent.

BREAKING THE 'PARENT' TRAP

Obviously, you have to be a parent for your children if you have any. But you do not have to parent yourself or your partner; you are adults and lovers, not parent and child. There are two main types of 'parent': the nurturing parent and the critical parent. If you feel that you have a tendency to take a parent role in your relationship, read through these sections and identify what type it is.

The Nurturing Parent

The nurturing parent typically disempowers themselves by

giving out the message, 'I am not enough for you just being myself, therefore I have to compensate.'

Think about it – if you make their meals, clean up after them, take responsibility for their issues, and meet all of their needs instead of yours, what are you saying? You are giving the implicit message that your needs are secondary to theirs and that neither you nor they need to prioritize you and your life. Therefore they won't remember to support you during a stressful work situation, or ever really look after you, because that has never been expected of them, or you have never communicated to them that this is necessary. Within your relationship, this leads to resentment on both sides.

Also, women or men who are particularly prone to playing the nurturing parent are often unconsciously attracted to partners who will take without feeling that they need to give anything in return – who are essentially quite selfish. This repeats a negative relationship pattern.

Breaking this pattern using the 'boundary exercise' in the previous chapter (*see pages 136–143*) should have given you some strategies that you can now continue to work on. Basically, you have to learn to put your needs on an equal footing to the needs of others.

Case Study | Carrie and Tom

Carrie had been married to Tom for ten years. Since moving to London five years earlier, they had both been very career-focused, and both had started to work late and put their careers first. However, over time Tom had put his heart and soul into his job. It had become his main identity, and he felt as though if he were successful in his job he was successful in his life. Carrie, meanwhile, had taken on the job of running the house and organizing all of their breaks and their holidays – holidays in which Tom invariably only ever managed to join her for half the time.

If they were due to go away for the weekend on Friday night, Tom would join her Saturday. If they had a ten-day holiday planned, Tom would join her for seven days. At first Carrie felt this made her independent and she had an image of them as a dynamic, busy couple, but gradually she realized that she was being completely taken for granted. Rather than them being equal partners, she was taking the role of the nurturing parent. She was enabling Tom to be completely focused on his job by providing a secure, nurturing base for him, but this wasn't happening the other way round. She had taught him it was acceptable to disregard her.

 TASKS FOR THE NURTURING PARENT

 These tasks will take 6 days.

There are four different task sections in this chapter, and each takes a different number of days. Basically, days 18–24 will be different depending on whether you are doing tasks identified for the parent or child ego state. For the nurturing parent ego state it is days 18–23, for critical parent it is days 18–24 and for rebellious and compliant child the tasks are on days 18–21. Read through the whole chapter before deciding which most applies to you.

Only do these exercises if you have identified yourself as a nurturing parent in the relationship.

DAY 18

 *Couple's and Individuals' Task*

List all of the things – emotional, practical, physical, psychological, sexual, financial – you do for your partner (or you did for your last partner if you are not currently in a relationship) and then list all of the things they do for you. Are the lists equal – and not just in length, but in content?

For instance:

I do for partner:	**They do for me:**
Cleaning	Make me laugh
Cooking	Satisfying in bed
Emotional support	Send cute texts

If you do all of their cleaning and cooking and give them constant psychological support, whereas they make you laugh, are satisfying in bed and occasionally text you, this is not an equal partnership. Really *identify the inequality in your relationship.* If you find it hard to see this, think about how a good friend or someone who cares about you more than your partner would describe the relationship.

DAY 19

 Couple's Tasks

List all of the things you would like your partner to do for you. List all of the things you would like to stop doing for them that are included on your list from yesterday. Your aim is to make this a reality.

 Individuals' Tasks

Imagine your next relationship and list all of the things you would like your next partner to do for you. You are going to expect to get these things and therefore you probably will get them, as you will change from the start of your relationship. There will be no more nurturing parent.

What I would like them to do for me

Listen to how my day was at work

Take responsibility for some of the household chores

Make me dinner sometimes

Encourage us to go out and buy theatre tickets etc.

Give me nice compliments

Seem excited to see me

Help me get the car ready on cold mornings

Plan nice holidays and weekends away.

What I would like to stop doing

Share housework instead of doing it all. Or get a cleaner.

DAY 20

Discuss what you have written in your lists with your partner.

As Carrie found when she did this with Tom, this exercise is often met with surprise. Your partner may have been conditioned for so long into believing that your needs do not count that they can resent your sudden change in thinking, and they can resent your resentment at the situation. Which all adds up to a lot of resentment!

Therefore, discuss the resentment you will both be feeling and try to understand the other's point of view. Your partner probably did not realize there was a problem and is likely to be shocked. Also, you did let this build up. However, you do deserve a more equally nurturing relationship where you both provide a secure base for each other.

Case Study | Carrie and Tom

Carrie handled this exercise rather badly, by dumping all her resentment on Tom in one go.

Carrie: I am no longer going to do everything for you, and what is more, I want you to start making an effort and act like you care about 'us'.

Tom: What do you mean, you do everything for me? I do lots of things for myself and I do care about us. What are you saying – that I'm just a lazy bugger who does nothing? Why are you with me if you think so little of me?

It would have been better for her to handle the situation in this kind of way:

Carrie: Let's look at the household chores and divide them up, and see if we can make life easier for us both.

Then later:

Carrie: Do you know what would be lovely? If we could sometimes plan nice nights out for each other – say, once a month – and take it in turns to surprise each other.

DAY 21

 Couple's Task

Devise (preferably with your partner) a strategy for all the things you would like your partner to do for you and see if you can mutually agree to it.

For example: 'I would like you to make me feel like a valued equal in this relationship. To do this, I'd like you to get home early at least two evenings a week so we can spend two quality evenings together, when we share the evening chores, such as cooking, but also spend some proper time together.'

Individuals' Task

Decide how you are going to play it next time, what you will expect from your future partner and yourself. Make a list of the things you are going to expect and a strategy for how to get them.

Expect	Strategy
Respect and care	Don't give in to 'midnight booty calls' after they have been out with their friends

DAY 22

 Couple's and Individuals' Tasks

Strengthen your resolve to stick to this. All of these exercises will ultimately be pointless if you lose your resolve. If you do not follow through on these resolutions, you are giving yourself and your partner the clear message that 'This is just a phase I am going through and can be disregarded. So carry on as though I never said anything.'

In order to strengthen your resolve, write yourself a letter detailing all you have resolved to do and agreed on in the last six days, and all the reasons why it is important that you keep to these changes. Whenever you feel you are slipping back into nurturing parent mode, re-read your letter.

DAY 23

 Couple's and Individuals' Tasks

Do the task below. If you are not currently in a relationship, apply it to your other social relationships like family and friends.

✎ Your Red/Green Diary

In order to check you are starting off as you mean to continue, I would like you to keep a red/green diary for the next three days. This means writing down each section of your day – for instance, Sunday morning – and then deciding whether it was 'green' or 'red'. Highlighting it with a green pen means that you and your partner were equally nurturing and kind to each other. You did not do more for them than they did for you. Highlight it in red if the balance is still unfair – for instance, you initiated sex, you got the papers, you made brunch, then you cleaned up. If you are not currently in a relationship, highlighting in a green pen means you felt your friends/colleagues/family did things for you during the interaction. Highlighting in red means you are the only one really making an effort.

At the end of three days, look at all of the red sections and devise a strategy for how to make them green for next week. For instance, next time you could wait for your partner to go and get the papers, even if it means going without for three days. Make a stand until they realize this task is up to them!

Case Study | Carrie and Tom

Luckily for Carrie and Tom, as they followed these exercises Tom realized how much he had expected from Carrie without attempting to return it. He also realized that his main barrier towards an equal relationship was his fear of losing his job, which is why he continuously put it first. Tom decided he had to do some work on this for himself in order to achieve a more even work/life balance.

DEALING WITH A RESISTANT PARTNER

However, there can be a problem when someone actually wants a mother rather than a partner. This person may be really resistant to change, because you have made their life so easy up until now. You have probably compensated for some of their faults and even their neglect of you. In order to deal with this level of resistance you are really going to have to be strong and say you do not want the relationship to continue if it means you are always going to be the one doing the nurturing. Why should you always take care of both of you? Where is your support?

Recognizing When It's Time to Go

If you still feel there is strong resistance, at this point you have to make a decision. If you truly want a supportive relationship, it may mean that you have to leave your current relationship so you can work on yourself in order not to equate feeling *needed* with feeling *loved*. And thereby allow yourself the possibility of meeting someone who is capable of supporting you. So after you have worked through these exercises, discussed your feelings with your partner and given them a chance to change (a one-month trial is enough time; any longer will induce complacency) – if after all this your partner is still showing no signs of supporting you, the chances are that they never will and it is probably time to go.

THE CRITICAL PARENT

When we are behaving like parents to our partners we are not always nurturing. Sometimes we are critical. In some ways this parental ego state is more damaging than the nurturing parent. At least when you are acting as a nurturing parent towards your partner you are behaving in a caring way – albeit one that is probably too much for yourself or them. However, when you are acting as a critical parent you are being overly critical towards yourself or your partner, and this is much harder to deal with.

The critical parent typically makes life very hard on themselves and those they are with, simply by the amount of pressure they exert on themselves and their partner in everyday life. Everyone has heard of the 'having it all syndrome' – aspiring to a perfect relationship, perfect family, perfect career, perfect house, perfect social life and perfect looks. Well, the critical parent has internalized these impossibly high standards and lives as though they are achievable – but with a bitter twist. Whenever they achieve anything, they move the goal posts and want to do better still, without ever celebrating what they have got. This makes them bitter with themselves and with others. They basically reject themselves, which means others reject them too. After all, how can you be in love with a constantly negative and critical person?

Are You a Critical Parent?

If you suspect you might have more than an element of 'critical parent' in you, have a look at the following. Have you ever:

- been really looking forward to seeing your partner at the end of the day and intending to be kind and loving, but instead finding yourself almost immediately criticizing something about them – their mess/ looks/ ability or lack of it/their time-keeping and so forth?

- found yourself shouting about something that is not even that important to you?

- found yourself complaining about your partner in front of people and embarrassing both them and yourself?

- asked them about their day and then told them how they should have done things without really just listening to them?

- received a present, such as a bunch of flowers, and thought how cheap carnations look?

- wanted to make an effort to look attractive for them but then giving yourself such a hard time about how bad you feel you look that you end up being angry with *them* because of the pressure you feel they put on you to look good?

If you have answered yes to any three of these, then you are functioning in a critical parent role. Basically, you put so much pressure on yourself, and then feel that you don't quite make the grade, that you end up spilling out your self-criticism onto others, particularly those you love the most. This really takes the joy from life. Remember the pessimistic personality described in the last chapter? Well, we all have a bit of that in us, or at least the capacity to be a bit like that in our relationship. This pessimistic bit can find a fault with anything. It can make us feel that we are never good enough, or any situation good enough.

A pessimist can be taken to a lovely restaurant for Valentine's Day but tell themselves it does not mean as much as it should have, because they had to remind their partner it was a special day. And that is the only reason their partner wanted to do something. A pessimist can ruin anything for themselves by criticizing it, and this can become impossible for a partner to have to live with.

Case Study | Veronique

Veronique had incredibly high standards for herself and those around her. Her last relationship ended because her partner was afraid of commitment and took a job that was 85 per cent travel. So the relationship fizzled out. Veronique blamed herself completely. She decided that the reason he stopped wanting to be in the relationship was something to do with her not being good enough. She had absolutely no understanding that it might have failed because of his issues; in her mind it was totally her fault. Basically, she was her own totally critical parent. This meant that in all her relationships she judged everything she did as either good or bad. She lived in a black-and-white world under mountains of pressure.

To stop this you need to follow these exercises for one week. Only do these if you have identified yourself as a critical parent in the relationship.

✎ TASKS FOR THE CRITICAL PARENT

🕐 These tasks will take 7 days.

👥 👤 *Couple's and Individuals' Task*

Take a small notebook everywhere you go and throughout the day write down every critical thought you have, whether it is about you or about someone else.

For instance: You are running late for one appointment so you think to yourself, 'You are always so late and never, ever organized.'

You catch sight of yourself and think, 'Gosh, you are fat; you must stop eating like a pig.'

You meet a friend for lunch and think they could do with wearing a bit more make-up, they look shattered.

DAY 19

👥 👤 *Couple's and Individuals' Tasks*

Read this list and divide it into what you say to yourself and what you say to others.

For instance: From the above list you can see that you have a tendency to generalize every little thing. So running late for one meeting means you see yourself as always so disorganized. This leaves you no space not to be perfect all the time. As no-one can be perfect all the time, the writer of this list is setting themselves up for constant criticism and self-rejection.

Similarly, just catching an unflattering glimpse of your reflection in a shop window can result in a huge name-calling tirade which is way over the top and really quite bullying.

Finally, instead of seeing the positive in things, like, 'Isn't it nice to be meeting a friend for lunch?' you appraise how you look and how they look negatively rather than sympathetically. Rather than thinking, 'Poor X, they are tired,' you think, 'She should wear more make-up.'

Look at what you say to yourself and decide whether you would ever say that out loud to someone else you cared for. The answer is, you probably wouldn't. If you did, they wouldn't want you around any more. Well, that is exactly what has happened – you don't want yourself around any more. So the chances are your relationships don't last. Just as you have rejected yourself, your partners will end up rejecting you and your constant criticism.

DAY 20

 Couple's and Individuals' Task

Look at the things you say to others and decide whether or not you really have a right to say them. Why do you constantly voice your negative opinions? Aren't you just imposing them on others? Every time you are about to say something critical, ask yourself, 'Is this really worth saying, or am I just being mean?'

DAY 21

Couple's and Individuals' Task

In response to the list you have made of all the negative things you say to yourself, come up with your own mantra, to be used to answer back to your critical voice.

Here are examples of some mantras in response to the critical parent voice described above:

'I am kind to myself. It's okay to be good enough. I don't need to be perfect.'

'Just one mistake does not mean I am always making mistakes.'

'Everyone is allowed to make mistakes.'

'I see the good in myself and others.'

Create Your Own Mantra

Mantras sometimes get a negative press. It is easy to dismiss them as ridiculously quick fixes to complex problems dreamt up by the positive-thinking gurus. However, if you can create your own mantra, one that really works for you, it could be the answer to your habit of self-criticism and could really help you turn your negative thoughts around.

Think about it: All that self-criticism and other critical thinking originates in your head. It comes out of your thoughts, but don't you have control over these thoughts? We often forget we can control what we think because life has sometimes made us forget we can. The fact is that you can reclaim that control by bringing your unconscious thinking into your conscious mind – by becoming aware of it.

You can start by rejecting the idea that you always need to be critical. Life is not all bad; just as we have the capacity to see the bad in everything, we also have the capacity to see the good. These mantras remind us that we don't always have to be critical. We can make our protective voices a little louder so at least we answer our critical voice. So you need to think of your own mantra. If I think of one for you, without knowing the content of your critical voice, it will not work nearly as well.

For instance, Veronique used the mantra, '*I don't have to be this critical, so I don't have to listen to this,*' every time she found herself being self-critical. And will it work? Yes – but you will have to do it consciously and consistently at first. It will take about 60 critical thoughts to be immediately answered back before your critical parent starts to be well and truly silenced. And it is most important to make sure that your mantra doesn't collude with your critical voice.

For example, maybe you have a habit of chastising yourself for being lazy: 'I am so lazy.' If your positive mantra is 'I am not that lazy,' you are giving yourself the message that the critical voice has a point, rather than rejecting it completely. Once you have given yourself an appropriate mantra to repeat, and are implementing it whenever you need to, you will develop your own protective voice. This will help you like yourself a bit more, which will encourage others to like and value you too.

Couple's and Individuals' Tasks

Your Red/Green Diary

Keep a **red/green diary** for the next two days. Every time you say something critical to yourself, or to others, describe what you said and why you said it, then highlight it in red. For every section of the day you weren't critical, mark it in green.

In the evening, review your diary. Look at the reds. Decide whether or not the criticism was worth it – was the shirt he was wearing really worth complaining about? Would you rather have had a nice time together or that he wore a different shirt? In order for you to be good to be around, the constant criticism has to stop, so decide only to allow yourself one complaint (red) all day. So use your criticism only when absolutely necessary.

DAY 24

 Couple's and Individuals' Task

Last, write yourself a letter reminding yourself why you are doing this and why it is so important to keep to your 'one red a day' strategy. Re-read it whenever your resolve weakens.

If you feel you fit into neither parent role, perhaps you take the role of child?

THE CHILD

The first interactions with others that we experienced were as children. We were children the first time we ever stood up for ourselves in the playground, or the first time we ever let someone else push us around a bit. These early experiences can be absolutely formative and often have lasting impact on how we behave for the rest of our lives. As adults, we can sometimes return to the position we know best when it comes to difficult interactions – the child. However, what worked for us as children may not work for us as adults.

An example of this is a client I worked with whom I shall call Rosie.

Case Study | Rosie

Rosie's father was an alcoholic and he often beat his wife and his children. Rosie learnt that if she hid behind the sofa her father would not find her and she would escape the kind of beating that no four-year-old should ever have to endure. Her mother would have needed a lot of support to leave her father but she never managed to get it, so she stayed in the abusive marriage. Rosie had to adapt and learn to protect herself as best as she could.

Rosie grew up and also married a violent drunk. Tragically, she was only repeating what she knew. She had learnt the victim mentality from her mother. (This is not a criticism of her, but a description of her state of mind.) And when her husband came home drunk and violent she dealt with it as she had as a child – she hid behind the sofa. It had worked as a child but it failed her most harmfully as an adult. To free herself from this appalling situation, Rosie was forced to learn how to think as an adult, rather than a helpless child.

On another note, the child ego state comes out of us every time we stamp our feet at something not going our way, or we think our friends are closer to each other than to us. Again, this playground jealousy is something all adults are capable of – even when we have been out of the playground for decades. We commonly call it paranoia.

Like behaving like a nurturing parent, a bit of child ego state can do us all good. We can laugh louder, dance more freely, play harder, get more excited, and lose our inhibitions as a child. Kept in balance, having childlike moments can be a gift. But taken to the extreme, they can make us foolish, naïve or just plain ridiculous. The child ego state works for children but the same state in adults typically makes us act either too rebelliously and defensively, or, at the other end of the scale, too compliantly.

Do You Behave Like a Child?

Have you ever:

- been upset about something in your relationship and had a lucid point to make in your head, but instead ended up yelling at your partner to 'Go to hell and you are an awful lover and I do not know why I put up with you'?

- screamed that the relationship is over and stormed out of the door, hoping they will follow you?

- got drunk together in a bar and then become convinced (paranoid) that they are flirting with other people, resulting in you causing a scene in the middle of the bar – perhaps even throwing your drink at them (in extreme circumstances)?

- said you will be home by one in the morning, then rocked up at four, with the defensive attitude of 'I don't care, they cannot tell me what to do'?

- flirted with a friend of theirs, or with a stranger in front of them, just to make them jealous?

- done something you know they really disapprove of, such as smoke or drink behind their backs, with a sense of freedom, because they do not know you're doing it, so you can?

- been unfaithful just to break a relationship rule?

If you have answered yes to any three of these, you are acting in rebellious child mode.

THE REBELLIOUS CHILD

Every time we shout or swear in an argument, we are presenting ourselves as a petulant child rather than an assertive adult. As a rule, the minute you shout in an argument, you have lost, even if you think you have won. You have let yourself down and shown you need to use brute force to make your point. Think about it: the most skilled arguers – barristers – would never shout or swear in a courtroom. Instead they advocate, listen and persuade.

Acting as a rebellious child does not empower you to put across your point assertively. Perhaps you want to smoke but your partner is against it. Instead of explaining that it is your life and your health and you will try to give up for yourself when you want to, you sneak cigarettes in exactly the way the naughty school child does, behind the bike sheds!

The rebellious child can become a rebel without a cause. So you end up sabotaging your relationship, and in turn hurting yourself, just for the sake of it. Or you are unfaithful for no other reason than to do something unhealthy to your relationship, destroying the trust you both shared, as well as your faith in yourself. Behaving like a rebellious child can be a symptom of not knowing how to be adult or of something more – of not believing you deserve to like yourself and be valued.

If you don't feel you deserve to be respected, then you won't act in a way that merits respect. This in turn lowers your self-image, so you end up feeling even more as though you don't deserve respect, and so it continues in a very vicious circle.

Case Study | Jeremy

Jeremy was a good man but he did not know how to handle conflict as an assertive adult. Instead he always resorted to behaving like a rebellious child, to the point of literally hitting his way out of an emotional or psychological corner. He would then direct all his remorse and shame inwards, which further destroyed his self-esteem and his relationships.

Through therapy, Jeremy began to see that the reason he resorted to his inner rebellious child was that this was the first ego state in which he had ever experienced and handled conflict. Once he stopped criticizing himself for being childlike, he was able to give himself the head space he needed to think about *not* using it. This makes sense, because if you chastise your rebellious side for being rebellious, the very fact it is rebellious will mean you continue to interact in this style to rebel against the telling-off you just gave yourself! A vicious circle that can only be broken by understanding, letting go, and having the faith that you can defend yourself when necessary without being constantly on the defensive.

The reason people interact in rebellious child mode is because they are used to it. If early-life arguments with parents, best friends, school mates and teenage dates were won by resorting to, 'I hate you, why can't you be on my side for once?' – reminiscent of the tantrum of an eloquent six-year-old – then we tell ourselves that this is the best way to communicate if we want to win an argument.

It is also fundamentally a lazy argument style. Defaulting to rebellious child mode does not require any lucid thought or real reflection about what we feel and how we want to communicate. Thinking and reflecting about what we want to say requires getting in touch with our feelings as an adult, rather than resorting to, 'I am upset, I have been unfairly treated, I will shout.' Arguments in rebellious child mode are also more likely to result in one or other partner leaving momentarily, or verbally ending the relationship, or criticizing our lover's vulnerabilities, or otherwise generally taking the relationship over the boundary of intimacy and caring and into the realms of damage. One of the main defences against stopping this negative interacting persona is fear of being hurt by the other. It almost becomes a question of pride – who can shout the loudest or hurl the most vicious insults? Just as with the argument rut, this will ultimately result in unhealthy or absent relationships.

 TASKS FOR THE REBELLIOUS CHILD

 These tasks will take 4 days.

Only do these exercises if you have identified yourself as a rebellious child.

 Couple's and Individuals' Task

Make a list all of the things you said in your last argument. This could have been with anyone; it does not need to be your partner.

For instance:

An argument you had with a friend

'You are such a selfish cow.'

'You totally use me.'

'I can't believe you are so lazy you can't even be bothered to come to my party.'

'You expect everyone to do everything for you but never do anything for anyone else.'

'Everyone thinks you are beyond selfish.'

DAY 19

 Couple's and Individuals' Tasks

Next to each item on the list, write the point you were trying to make without the attacking comments that accompanied it.

So, in your argument with your friend:

Your attacking comment	**What you were really trying to say**
You are such a selfish cow.	I am surprised you are not coming to my birthday.
You totally use me.	
I can't believe you are so lazy you can't be bothered to come to my party.	
You expect everyone to do everything for you but never do anything for anyone else.	I feel very let down as I would have thought we both prioritized supporting each other.
Everyone thinks you are beyond selfish.	I am hurt because I feel rejected, I need you to treat me the same way I treat you.

Remind yourself of this interaction checklist:

- Don't be defensive

- Don't be attacking

- Don't be rude

- Be clear

- Be assertive.

✎ BEING ASSERTIVE

This is such an important part of good communication and equal relationships, so let's just spend some time defining assertive communication.

When you communicate assertively, you make direct statements regarding your feelings, thoughts, and wishes. These should remind you of the golden rules for communications repeated throughout this manual. You stand up for yourself but also are aware of the person you are talking to, particularly your partner, whom you should be treating as your best friend. They are the most important person to you so you should treat them as such, and they should treat you as such too.

When you are being assertive, you listen to others and let them know you have heard them but you can also tell them what you think and need. You listen to what they are saying but not at the expense of your own rights, dignity and happiness. You can make both direct requests and direct refusals. You can start and stop a conversation without falling back into the argument rut. While you are being assertive you convey an air of maturity and rationality. You do not sound hysterical, aggressive or compliant. In order to convey this, keep your voice relaxed and of an even tone, speak strongly but do not shout, keep eye contact but do not stare, stand tall and do not clench your fists.

Re-read this list until you have committed it to memory.

DAY 20

Couple's and Individuals' Task

Think about the last time you felt you let yourself down. Write down in what way you did this and your motivation for doing it:

For instance:

What I actually did

Got upset they forgot to take out the bins again

Shouted

Ended the relationship

Called my partner lazy, selfish and a rubbish boyfriend

Told myself my relationship was awful and I would always have to do everything

Caused a bad feeling for 24 hours until I had to apologize and make up.

What I wish I had done

Realized they had not taken the bins out but kept the fact it was just the bins in perspective, and I am not going to lose control over rubbish, literally

Observed this to them calmly, directly, and not in a confrontational way

Kept my voice level

Told them I needed them to do this errand so that we both contributed to the house chores and it was important for me not to feel taken for granted, and that they did something to contribute

Remind them that this upsets me as we can't put the bins out for another week and it is, at least, an inconvenience

Then moved on, as we both understood the interaction. So no actual argument happened over the bins.

DAY 21

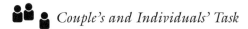 *Couple's and Individuals' Task*

Write yourself a letter outlining how you wish to communicate and act from now on.

Remember, this is not an extreme exercise. One little blip does not mean you should abandon this attempt to heal yourself completely.

THE COMPLIANT CHILD

The child ego state is not only about extreme aggression or rebellion. It can also mean being too compliant and passive in some cases. Remember Rosie. This ego state can be equally destructive.

'Yes, dear,' when not really listening is the response of the stereotypical male character coping with a nagging (*critical parent*) wife. But the 'Yes, dear' syndrome exists in many modern and supposedly equal partnerships. How many people agree to something in the moment, when in reality they are thinking they will never do that or they will subversively try and change their partner's minds later, or just plain pretend to forget? The compliant child persona adopts the view that it is easier to agree. But is it?

Agreeing to something for the sake of a peaceful life causes unconscious resentment to build up and life becomes more forced than truly peaceful. The compliant child is the type of person who feels as though they are constantly walking on eggshells. The compliant child can also feel as though they have lost their own sense of identity, as they are so used to simply agreeing with their partner's plans, ideas, preferences and general way of living.

The compliant child almost seeks to keep their partner by offering no resistance to them and they typically really fear facing confrontation. This sounds as though the compliant child is setting themselves up to be the victim in the relationship, and this is sometimes the tragic case. But their persona can also stem from a lack of motivation to make decisions for themselves, and not enough self-awareness to know what they like and therefore to be able to champion their own views.

ARE YOU A COMPLIANT CHILD?

Have you ever:

- found yourself out on a night with your partner, wishing you were anywhere but there?

- found yourself being yelled at by your partner and hanging your head in embarrassment, accepting everything they say?

- lending them money that you resent giving them because you know you will never see it again?

- being left at home to babysit while they go out, thereby not allowing you to go out for the second time that week?

- turning a blind eye to infidelity yet again?

- changing your clothes because they tell you to?

- having a relationship with an attached man and just hoping for the best, not asking him to commit?

- saying you don't mind in answer to a question when actually you really do have a preference?

If you have answered yes to three or more you are acting like a compliant child in this relationship.

Compliant child roles within a relationship often result in you not demanding any respect or any acknowledgement of your needs, tragic if it is only because you fear conflict. Unsurprisingly, this means you are not given any respect, and your needs are not prioritized. You do not give the message of being 'easy-going' or 'easy to love and low maintenance'; rather you give the message of being undeserving of your partner and 'lucky to have them'. If you act like this, then they will begin to think that is actually the case – that you really do not deserve them and that they can take you for granted.

Behaving like this is obviously not conducive to a secure and supportive relationship. You need to ask yourself, 'Why am I acting as if I do not deserve kindness?' If you genuinely think you do not, then what negative, and perhaps abusive, patterns are you repeating? Were you rejected by a parent, lover or friend? If so, in order not to hate them and to prove them right in their rejection of you, you then have to coerce rejection in all of your subsequent relationships. But wouldn't it be easier just to recognize that the parent/lover/friend was wrong to reject you in the first place? If you can accept that it was their fault that they missed your intrinsic valve you will start to prevent, rather than to embrace, any further painful relationships.

  TASKS FOR THE COMPLIANT CHILD

These tasks will take 4 days.

Only do the following tasks if you have identified yourself as a compliant child in your relationship.

 Couple's and Individuals' Tasks

Make a list what you like to do in your free time.

Make a list of the type of clothes you like to wear, the food you like to eat.

Write about who you are. The following is fairly typical of the kind of list clients produce with me in therapy:

> Sociable
> Funky dresser, but not bothered about labels
> Like Thai food

Like films
Want a career but also want to travel
Adventurous
Extrovert
Not worried about commitment
Like living alone
Like dating partner
Not family-orientated.

Now check to make sure the list is about you, not about you and your partner.

Case Study | Jake

Jake broke up from his girlfriend of three years and promptly gave up his rented flat. He realized that having such a flashy home was not such a priority for him that it justified his spending most of his disposable income on it. He told me, 'I realized I lived there for the image my girlfriend wanted me to project, not the image I wanted.' Jake had slipped into compliant child mode – living his life to suit someone else's dreams. If you do this, how can your relationship have the respect necessary for its survival?

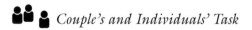 *Couple's and Individuals' Task*

Look at your lists and analyze how easy it was to draw them up.

For example, look again at the list you just made in the above exercise. Now think about whether you have lost your sense of identity to such an extent you don't know what makes you happy any more? Have you lost your identity by taking on the identity of your partner and in doing so lost the reasons why you were valued and why you valued yourself in the first place?

The writer of the list above identified that:

Sociable
Funky dresser but not bothered about labels
Likes Thai food
Likes films
Wants a career but also wants to travel
Adventurous
Extrovert

… were all traits that really did describe her.

However:

Not worried about commitment
Likes living alone
Likes dating partner
Not family-orientated

… were more about her partner than about her. She was adventurous and wanted to travel but she did not think this excluded them moving in together for now, or making future plans. She liked spontaneity but did not think this needed to exclude security. She was trying to convince herself she felt like this so she could comply with her boyfriend.

 *Couple's and Individuals' Task*

The trick here is that each time you do something, ask yourself, 'Do I really want to do this?' The reason this empowers you is because it helps you to remember what it is like to listen to yourself, to know yourself and to make up your own mind.

So perhaps you find yourself thinking, 'I really want to stay in tonight.' Ask yourself, 'Do I really, or am I doing it to please ...? If I had the choice to do anything different, would I?'

Go over this task with your partner and ask them for their support, not their permission. As with all the tasks, if they are unwilling to support you, then you have to ask yourself whether or not your relationship is worth healing, or whether you need to heal yourself and leave the relationship.

Taking the role of the compliant child may have been appropriate at one time in your life, but as an autonomous adult it will drain you and leave you lost in a submissive, rather than a healthy, relationship with yourself and with your partner.

If you have got to here without identifying yourself as ever acting in any one of these ego states, go back and re-read this chapter and re-think. You would not be buying this book if one of these ego states did not resonate with you, and indeed they can all briefly resonate with all of us at one time or another.

THE RATIONAL ADULT

A lot of this book so far has been aimed at helping you access your adult state. This is because we are trying to help you have a functioning, healthy relationship between two consenting adults. 'Adult' is the key word here – you don't want to be a parent or child, you want to be a lover, partner, friend, and adult man or adult woman with your loved one.

The aim of all of these tasks has been to achieve this, and if you have followed everything so far you should be on your way to functioning in this ego state. Still, it never hurts to have another summary.

HOW AN ADULT BEHAVES ...

- As a rational adult you will be assertive rather than aggressive. Therefore, as I described in Chapter 5, looking at the argument rut, you don't scream, shout or throw a tantrum in an argument. Rather, you explain your point calmly. Further, the points you bring up are valid and not symptoms of your insecurities.

- As an adult you are not defensive. Instead, you let your partner have an opinion as long as it is constructive. You are also comfortable to express your own opinions.

- As an adult you have a balance in your relationship – a balance not only with the effort you both put in, but with the time you spend together as opposed to the time you spend apart. You feel more valued than your partner's career, financial and material things, and they similarly feel valued by you. You feel more valued than their friends and family, and vice versa. This may sound utopian, but if it does you are not in a truly appreciative and happy relationship.

- As an adult you value your own sexuality and therefore want a sex life that fulfils your needs – though again, a balance has to be achieved. You both want to have a satisfying sex life but that does not mean either of you has to compromise yourself or do something you are really uncomfortable with.

- As an adult you have a balance between working towards your own dreams, your partner's dreams, and your shared dreams, and living for today. Do not save everything for a rainy day only to realize it has been raining for a long time in your relationship.

- As an adult you value yourself and this healthy relationship you are trying to create, and if it is truly healthy your partner will value it too.

- As an adult you act in an assertive, calm way. You are unafraid of returning someone's gaze, you have control over what you say, so you do not unnecessarily hurt those you are talking to. You are direct and can express your needs, but can also listen to the needs of those you care about. You meet only the appropriate needs and know how to define appropriateness.

- As an adult, you can be joyful and sad but in a balanced way. You are grounded and emotionally mature. You do not overreact. You recognize and respect your own personality style. You do not catastrophize. You are not overly compliant and you know how to be protective of yourself.

I hope by now you will be reading this and understanding how you are going to relate, interact, and love from now on. You need to be determined to have an adult relationship.

The bottom line is that only by loving, accepting and respecting yourself will you be able to love, accept and respect your partner in a truly adult relationship.

TO SUM UP ...

This chapter is a type of map of the ego states we can all have. You should by now have identified in which particular state you were functioning. You will have undertaken the tasks set out over the week at just 20 minutes a day, tasks designed to neutralize the more destructive effects of the dysfunctional ego states.

You will then have read about how the rational adult functions and resolved to try and adopt this in the main. We are aiming here for *most of the time*. Blips don't destroy relationships – we are all only human – but continuous destructive patterns and ego states do.

So let's just quickly review all of the changes we've made in the last three weeks:

- You have committed to working through this book

- You have built up some trust with your partner

- You have discovered why you argue

- You have imposed argument management techniques

- You have introduced rational discussion

- You have identified your own and your partner's personality style

- You have a greater understanding of how these personality styles can compensate for, or conflict with, each other

- You have identified your destructive ego state

- You are both working towards functioning in your adult ego states.

That's quite a lot of change in just over three weeks. By now you should be recognizing some profound changes in your relationships. The next week is about making your relationship the best it can be. After all, who wants an okay relationship? We all really want perfect relationships – at least most of the time.

CHAPTER 9

ACTING THE PART
Practical Ways to Improve Your Relationship

Let's face it, you don't want to have to have heart-to-hearts every other day after finishing this book – so what other daily techniques can help a relationship, apart from communication?

As I said in the first chapter, none of us is going to have a perfect relationship all of the time – that would be totally unrealistic. What we are aiming for in this book is a relationship that brings more pleasure than pain. Thus far, we have looked at how to handle tricky situations as they occur. We have worked on re-building the trust between you and increasing your empathy with each other. We have examined how you can stop arguments before they start and address their underlying causes. We have shown how understanding your personality and that of your partner can make your relationship happier. We have seen how you and your partner can either complement each other, or have the potential to destroy each other.

We have also looked at how we all need to take appropriate responsibility for ourselves and our own behaviour. And how we can function as rational adults with emotional maturity and appropriate assertiveness within our relationships. So we have really looked at how to face, prevent and resolve conflict.

All these factors are vital for happy relationships. But there is more you can do. This chapter is about giving the day-to-day life within your relationships the best possible chance of being calm or fun rather than draining. In this chapter we are going to look at what you can do in *practical* ways to increase the warmth and closeness you feel during the already good times. In other words, how you can make your relationship even better, even warmer and even stronger.

THE INTERPLAY OF THOUGHT, EMOTION AND ACTION

Our emotions affect our thoughts, which affect our behaviour. If we are in an angry mood, we are likely to be irritated by the smallest thing, from the time it takes the Tube to arrive to what our partner says as we walk through our front door. These small things make us even angrier still, until we feel we have been pushed into losing our temper – when in reality we pushed ourselves into losing our reason.

This interplay of emotion, thought, and action can happen in any order. For example, we can think something randomly, such as, 'People are giving me funny looks on this bus,' and then feel absolutely insecure and paranoid that we look out of place when there is no logical reason for this. But the thought makes us want to hide – or at least go home and change, which are irrational emotions and actions stemming from a random thought.

In the same way, if we look at the floor and meet no-one's eye as we are walking down the street, we can almost convince ourselves that everyone is staring at us. Try it. By your actions, you can make yourself feel vulnerable. So what comes first – behaviour, feeling or thought? And does it actually matter? As I explained earlier, if we want to act maturely, then we ultimately need to make our thoughts consciously control and influence our emotions, which is a very subtle thing to manage. So I suggest you try and change that over which you have most control – your actions.

Act as though you respect yourself, look after yourself, and listen to your own needs. If you don't want to go to the pub with your boyfriend, don't. If you are out with your friend, don't get so drunk that you behave destructively and end up causing an argument or a crisis. If you're in an argument, don't shout but speak to be heard. Soon you will begin to realize you can behave in a way that shows you respect yourself and you deserve respect from others. You will begin to think that actually you do deserve some respect and even experiencing this thought should help you feel better about yourself.

GETTING PRACTICAL

The practical aspects of a relationship should never be ignored. After all, it is unrealistic to think you would be able to, or want to, have intense conversations all the time – you would get fed up very soon!

The practicalities I want to focus on are:

- body language

- compliments

- quality time

- fun.

In this chapter, we are going to put into practice some very simple body language tasks, to help you and your relationship feel as secure, and to help you build as much confidence, as possible.

Nothing attacks our self-confidence like an insecure relationship. If we start each day not feeling appreciated by our partner, we will continue it by not appreciating ourselves. So let's really look at this process now by taking one typical experience we all have, and analyzing how different interactions around this one experience can produce dramatically different results in terms of the way it makes us feel.

The Situation:
Getting ready to go to work, saying goodbye to our partner and leaving the house.

This is a really simple, almost mundanely uncomplicated situation. It is so everyday and normal it can hardly impact upon our lives – can it? In fact it can, very much so. It is precisely within the everyday and the mundane that most psychological damage is done, and, more to the point, this damage often goes entirely unnoticed.

I'm now going to run through several variations on how the way you and your partner interact during this simple situation can severely impact on your state of mind for the rest of the day. For ease of writing I am using an example of a 'him' criticising a 'her', but this works for anybody in any intimate relationship.

Variation 1:

You get dressed to go to work. Your partner says nothing and doesn't comment on the effort you have made with your appearance. In fact, he hardly turns his head to return the goodbye kiss you have initiated as you leave the house.

You may not even realize this, but as you walk out of the house and down the street you will be missing the warm glow of a satisfying relationship and the feeling of being loved, which leaves you just that little bit exposed to the elements.

Variation 2:

Your partner in some way criticizes your appearance, which makes you think maybe you are too scruffy, or overdressed, or whatever other depreciating message he gave you, and although he kisses you goodbye, it is perfunctory and cold.

You leave the house, shut the door behind you, and start your journey to work already criticizing the way you dress, or the way you let your partner get away with his criticism. Either way, you have started criticizing yourself before you even get to work and start the minefield of your day. You are not just exposing yourself to disappointment; you are positively vulnerable to further chips at your self-esteem.

Variation 3:

You get dressed in silence and as you or your partner leaves, you or he shouts goodbye at the front door without bothering to kiss goodbye. You or he then continues to get ready.

This routine is normal and not particularly painful, but it is numbing. If you and your partner make no acknowledgment of each other, as you shut your door and turn to face the outside world you will already feel numbed to the routine nature of life. You will feel like a little cog in a big wheel, invisible even to the one person who is supposed to value you above all else.

Variation 4:

You get dressed while occasionally chatting to your partner. He comments on how lovely you look and as you properly kiss each other goodbye with attention and intention, you genuinely wish each other a good day. You shut the door, checking you both have your keys so you can get back in later – a bit of nurturing parent creeping in, as long as this is balanced it is no bad thing.

As you walk down the road, probably thinking of something entirely different, without realizing it you have already been validated and your self-esteem will be boosted.

Obviously, Variation 4 is the one we all want. In order to get it, we could get rid of unsupportive partners. Or, as that is probably a little extreme, we could change the way we act in order to affect the way they react to us. The truth is that we have more control over the messages we receive than we think. In fact we can control the messages we receive by monitoring the messages we give out.

THE IMPORTANCE OF BODY LANGUAGE

Most of our communication is non-verbal; it is transmitted through our body language. Body language tells people how we feel about ourselves and invites them to clarify that position for us. If we give out the message that we are unsure most of the time, people will respond to us as though we really are unsure. If we give out the message that we feel good about ourselves, or at least a little bit confident, we will be treated as confident people. Let's call this the *positive position*. We give out the message that we expect positive feedback and mostly, therefore, we get it. This positive feedback then boosts our confidence, which means we give out more messages that we feel confident and we get more supportive and confidence-building messages back, in an entirely virtuous and boosting pattern.

✎ Getting to a Positive Position

Let's look at our everyday leaving-the-house situation again.

When you get dressed, if you tell yourself you look good and see the positives of any look (even the 'nothing left clean but this' outfits), you naturally begin to feel positive about yourself. There is a way of doing this:

Technique 1:

When you are ready, take a look in the mirror. Put your shoulders back and down, stand tall and stand straight. Don't lean away from the mirror as though repulsed by your reflection and really see yourself as a whole – not just the bags under your eyes or the annoying spot but *you* – the effort you have made, the positive things about your face, your figure and your clothes. Then smile at yourself and mentally give yourself a compliment.

Why do this?

This will have a buffering effect on your self-esteem similar to that of Variation 4, where your partner compliments you. Here, you will compliment yourself before you even say goodbye to your partner. So when you approach that interaction you are giving out the message, 'I feel positive,' which, as we have already discovered, invites positive feedback about the way you look.

Give Yourself Some Compliments

Now let's add some verbal techniques to our non-verbal cues. Body language does a lot, but words also help. The words we use give out messages on two main levels: one level is the content or information we intend to share and the other is how we are actually feeling about that subject, about the person we are talking to, and about ourselves. The words we use are not only messages to the other person, they are also messages to ourselves.

Technique 2:

When you are leaving, go up to your partner and give them a goodbye kiss. Tell them to have a good day, and say something positive about yourself, such as, 'I feel that I am going to have a good day today as I had a good night's sleep and feel relaxed and positive. Plus I really like this new outfit.' Don't ask in a weak voice, 'How do I look?' which actually gives out the message that you expect criticism – you may just get what you ask for. Instead, find something positive to say about your partner and give them a compliment. This is not in order to get one back – fishing for compliments is something women are often accused of – rather it is to get the concepts of compliments re-introduced into your relationships.

As with anything you want more of in your life, you have to start by introducing it slowly. If compliments have become a thing of the past, then you can consciously try and bring them into the present. Even if the whole process starts off as being one-sided, it will eventually filter through.

GIVE YOURSELF SOME POSITIVE SPIN

Now that we've had a look at different variations of body language, let's move on to looking at how we present and compliment ourselves. Basically, we all make judgements about other people and they make judgements about us. This is nothing to fear as you don't have to care what people think of you – it's healthy not to most of the time. If you did, you would literally drive yourself mad worrying what everyone thought.

But we do – or should – care what our partner thinks. And we can influence this. I am not suggesting for one minute that you do everything your partner wants you to in order for them to think highly of you. First, this would not work. As we discussed when we looked at the nurturing parent and compliant child personalities, no-one respects anyone if they just continually people-please. Second, the aim of this book is not to encourage you to become a doormat, in fact quite the opposite. What I am suggesting is that as you care what your partner thinks of you, you should present the things you do in the best possible light.

It is absolutely fine to blow your own trumpet a little when you have done something well. This could be anything from resolving a conflict to doing a good workout. The important thing is to present these things about you positively rather than pessimistically. Basically, be your own fan and then others will be too.

In therapy, when presented with this theory, people often say, 'Well, I can't just make stuff up about me.' Maybe you are thinking that too, in which case you are slightly missing the point. I am not suggesting you lie or even embellish the truth but (*as I explained in the optimist section of Chapter 7*), you can see the same things either negatively or positively. I am asking you just to use your protective voice (*rather than your critical one, see Chapter 8*) to see what you did well in any situation and be pleased with yourself for just that. Then start to get into the habit of mentioning some of the good things you did or felt that day to your partner, so that you extend this way of seeing yourself in a positive light to them.

If we were watching TV and an advert came on saying something was just about okay, but no more than that, we might find the honesty refreshing, but we would be very unlikely to rush out and buy this mediocre product. The same goes for people and relationships. I am not suggesting that everyone should start becoming really arrogant and full of themselves, but unless they are naturally arrogant or in denial or delusional, people don't tend to be arrogant anyway. People are far more likely to be overly humble than arrogant – so let's not worry about this and focus instead on giving yourself some positive presentation.

STOP APOLOGIZING!

First, let's look at the way you talk. How we talk reflects how we feel about ourselves, how we are asking others to respond to us, and how we view the world. There is a simple way of looking at this: how many times do you apologize for yourself in a day? Think about it. Most people do it all the time. Have you ever had someone bump into you and yet you apologize to them! This is an everyday example of the way that we all take on the responsibility for someone else's mistakes and apologize for them ourselves. Moreover, we are often actively looking for ways we could be at fault, for situations where we need to apologize. This is a small example of 'blame culture', where every action requires a judgement and someone needs to take the blame.

We could apologize like this every single day on the street and it wouldn't really matter, but what if we did this all the time in our own relationship? It wouldn't destroy our relationship but it certainly won't make us feel as good as we could do, which in turn means our relationship won't feel as good as it could.

The changes we can make to improve this are small and within our everyday lives. We can start by saying 'Excuse me,' rather than 'Sorry' when we bump into someone accidentally, and accepting someone else's apologies when they bump into us. Basically, by doing this we stop accepting blame for things that are not our fault and, even more imperceptibly but equally importantly, we stop thinking about blame. Not everything needs blame; some things just are as they are. As we have already said, people naturally judge even when judgement is unnecessary. In our relationships we do the same.

Case Study | Mia and Tom

Back to our by-now-familiar Mia and Tom.

Tom came home from work and over dinner was telling Mia about a particularly tricky political situation at work that he had struggled with but ultimately felt he handled well. He was telling her to just touch base, as our relationships are often our secure base, and also because he cared about her, and therefore cared what she thought.

As he recounted the events, she kept interrupting him with comments like, 'Did you do so and so? Oh, I would have done it like this instead.' This caused Tom to feel unsupported, harshly judged, and negative towards Mia. This negativity was not entirely fair (nothing ever is in relationships), as Mia was just trying to support him as best she could. But she was being too critical as she was judging when no judgement was needed. The event had passed and they could not change that. However, if she had given support and just listened to him, perhaps adding, 'Oh, that was good …' she could have made Tom feel positive about himself and about his relationship with her. Then she could have said, 'If it happens again you could always try this as well

…,' thereby still getting her points across and helping Tom shape future interactions at work.

STOP THE BLAME GAME

In this case no judgement was needed. It couldn't change anything anyway. Couples always think establishing blame is important, but why? What will it change? Isn't it just better to think how best to move forward from the situation? In our relationships we can do this by sometimes letting things just be. For instance, whether or not tiny household tasks get done all the time doesn't really matter, if respect is given and no maliciousness is intended. Blame shouldn't be taken or assumed.

You can influence how you as a couple perceive an event by the positive or negative spin you put on it. Negative spin relates to blame. You can say, 'We had a huge row and it was all Lucy's fault,' or you can say, 'We had a row. Neither of us managed to bring it back and handle the problem maturely but we are going to try next time.' Arguments are hard, but if we put a negative spin on them we prolong and inflame them. For instance, you can say, 'That row was awful and will be hard to recover from, and what is more I am still blaming Lucy, so I'm psychologically continuing it.' Or you can say, 'It happened. We can't change it. But we are going to handle the aftermath as maturely and positively as possible.'

Case Study | Bettina

Bettina was feeling very angry with herself. She had just phoned her husband because she wanted some support over how long she had had to work away from home. Because her husband missed her, he was frustrated, and in that moment he was not supportive. Bettina sensed this and immediately responded by apologizing for asking for support, thereby adding some blame into the situation. Because she had apologized, her husband saw she was in some way taking the blame and so, because he felt blame was needed too, he then apologized. Although no argument happened, they both felt bad, with an inkling of being got at by the other.

If Bettina had stayed adult (*Chapter 7*) and recognized her partner was not voicing his real feelings but inadvertently showing how much he missed her and how insecure he was feeling (*Chapter 3*), she could have 'named' these feelings and they could have been nice to one another on the phone for support. Alternatively, Bettina's husband could have realized he was being defensive because he missed her (*Chapter 3*) and was therefore acting in rebellious child mode (*Chapter 7*). He was doing this because he missed her and not because he was cross with her. They could have healed the situation without introducing any negative spin or blame into the mix.

I'm not suggesting in this chapter that you have to judge everything as having a positive or negative spin before you say it, and that you should try and avoid the latter all of the time. Rather, I am trying to help you identify the almost unnoticed patterns in your everyday interactions so that you can then, over time, work on generally helping them become more positive. Ultimately, you may achieve a pattern in your relationship that is free from either unnecessary blame or judgement.

 TASKS TO HELP YOU PROJECT A POSITIVE SELF-IMAGE

These tasks will take 1 day.

Everyone starts and finishes at the same point in this chapter. So, as some people will be on day 25, let's start there.

DAY 25

Couple's and Individuals' Tasks

A good way to give something a 'positive spin' is by complimenting yourself or others, as by doing this you are bringing out the good in the situation. Compliments can be forgotten during stressful times, but these should be happening less often now that you know about conflict resolution and management. So now is a good time to bring compliments back into your relationship with enthusiasm.

Each day, make a conscious decision to compliment yourself. Do this first thing in the morning, before you leave the house, so you can create that happy bubble around yourself I described at the beginning of this chapter. Also, compliment your partner once a day too. Don't make this feel forced. Just put your positive spin on what they do and you will see something about them that feels worth complimenting. We see good when we look for it, so now you are going to ensure you look for it.

So your task is to look for the good at least twice a day – once for yourself and once for your partner. If you are doing this as a couple, that's four compliments a day – one each to yourselves and one to each other. And if you are doing this on your own, give yourself two compliments a day.

Next I would like you to start thinking about something extremely important, that many couples forget: having a good time in their relationship. This means making sure in practical terms that there is time for the relationship to be fun. You need to prioritize excitement and enjoyment within your relationship.

DON'T FORGET THE GOOD TIMES!

I know we have discussed getting the balance right in earlier chapters, but in this context we need to make sure we are having as much fun with our partner as we do with our friends. If you are reading this and thinking, 'Fun, what fun?' then your balance is definitely out and you need to inject some back into things right now.

Getting the Balance Right

Balance is when you make sure you spend quality time with your partner and they do the same for you. Unfortunately, an extension of taking your partner for granted, or them taking you for granted, is that they can spend all of their energy at work chasing a promotion up the career ladder, or on seeing their friends. This can make you feel that everyone else gets the best of them and you just get the rest of them. It can feel as though they only come to you to recover and be cared for, and when they are refreshed and energized again they leave you once more, in order to carry on with what they were doing, be it sport, job, socializing, or just about anything that does not involve you.

Expect Quality and Quantity

If this is the case you will not be getting any quality time with them. Or maybe you are reading this and thinking that when your partner reads this they will think this is exactly what *you* do, and feel really taken for granted. If you are working through this book on your own and thinking of your past relationships and trying to identify where they went wrong, perhaps you were the one not giving your partner quality time and tending to take them for granted. Or maybe you were left at home thinking that you did not feel valued. Either way, the techniques to remedy the situation remain the same.

Before we move on to the remedy, please remember that things do not need to be this way. There is a happy medium between the two extremes of either taking someone for granted and spending all of your best energy with people outside your relationship, or being the one constantly left feeling undervalued. Real life is about working with shades of grey as well as the black-and-white positions. So if you think you have a tendency not to have a balance of quality time at any point, please work through this. Something that starts off as an occasional problem can escalate into an extreme issue if left unchecked for a long period of time.

Case Study | Elizabeth and Wilson

Elizabeth and Wilson had been together for fourteen years, married for twelve, and they had two little boys. When they first met, Wilson was a high-powered banker and spent a lot of time at work chasing deals and bonuses – basically he sought recognition through his work. One of the things that made Elizabeth feel this might turn into a serious relationship when they first met was that he calmed down the amount of hours he worked in order to spend time with her. This made her feel special. Wilson stopped working weekends and they went out on a date at least once during the week. Wilson certainly made an effort to find a balance between his professional and personal life, possibly for the first time since university.

Once they were married he began again to chase more deals at work. It was as if his excitement at chasing a deal, which in this case had been getting Elizabeth to marry him, had waned now that he had achieved his goal. The imbalance started to creep back in; they still had 'date night' during the week, but he started to return home on the other nights later and later, and start work earlier and earlier. Elizabeth began to feel like she was simply supporting him to go to work, and her job was to have his shirts ready so that he could leave in the morning at six sharp. Elizabeth reasoned that this was having a beneficial effect on her career – because she woke up when he did, she could get lots of planning done as she did not have to be at work until two and a half hours later.

Once they decided to start a family it took some time to conceive, mainly because they were only having sex at weekends. Wilson was simply not there during the weeks. Then, when Elizabeth did get pregnant she inevitably felt more tired, especially with the early starts and the morning sickness. She felt less like going out on their regular Wednesday date night and preferred to stay in with Wilson, eating together, watching a movie or just talking. For Elizabeth this was like having a date night at home, but Wilson saw it more as just another night in and began to get back later and later from work on this night too.

Nothing was said at this time, perhaps because the changes were very gradual, but soon their evening together during the week had become lost and they simply had their relationship at weekends. Wilson reasoned he was providing for his future family and Elizabeth tried to reassure herself with this thought as well. During the latter stages of pregnancy, when they were staying in a lot more at weekends, Wilson started to 'just do five minutes of e-mailing' at weekends. This soon crept up to working whole mornings from home on Saturdays.

By the time their first baby was born, Wilson was spending all of his energy during the week at work, while taking calls and doing work on Saturdays. Sunday was family day. Elizabeth was busy looking after her new baby but the thought did start to occur to her that she was basically a single mother when it came to the care of this baby. Wilson did not bath his son until he was five weeks old, and he never, ever changed a nappy – he wasn't there enough. The slight imbalance when they first dated developed into negligence when they were married.

This remained the situation for a few years and they tried to compensate for it by having several family holidays a year. The problem was that they had no quality time together as a couple. They either had separation, with Wilson at work and Elizabeth at home caring for their son while working part time, or they had family time on Sundays and holidays. Although they socialized on Saturday nights, they had literally forgotten to factor in any couple time and counted socializing with friends and family or being just a family as their time together, when it wasn't. It was time with other people, which had become hugely imbalanced. By the time of the birth of their second child, Wilson had been fast-tracked in a big way and their material quality of life was fantastic, but they had almost no emotional quality of life at all. They stopped having sex after the birth of their second child and neither seemed to notice. Wilson worked Saturdays and Sundays from home. Elizabeth was feeling isolated and Wilson pressured.

Eventually, they woke up and realized they just co-existed, in the sense that although they shared a living space it was rarely at the same time. Effectively, they led two very different lives. Imbalance in the time they spent together had destroyed their emotional bond. They literally panicked and both fought very hard to bring the focus back to them as a couple.

✎ TASKS TO BRING SOME BALANCE BACK INTO YOUR RELATIONSHIP

🕐 These tasks will take 1 day.

DAY 26

👥 👤 *Couple's and Individuals' Tasks*

Make a timetable of how you spend your usual week. Be honest. Write what you do, not what you wish you did. So many people write that they go to the gym four times a week, rather than the actual two. Now divide your time into:

Time at work
Time on your own – exercising, shopping etc.
Time socializing with friends
Time spent with family
Time spent as a couple
Time spent recovering – vegging out, watching TV.

You should then devise a ratio so that work takes up no more than half your waking hours. Then, if you have children, your family time should be one third of your time and your couple time is half of the rest of the time:

Work	50 per cent
Family	33 per cent
Couple	8.5 per cent
Rest	8.5 per cent.

This is an absolute maximum guideline, in that work must never be more than 50 per cent, and if you can make it less, add in more time together as a couple and more time to yourself. If you are following this guideline, you will realize that 6 per cent is not a lot of time. It is just one evening a week. So try and compensate for this by having at least one weekend away, or one holiday with just the two of you, as a couple, per year. If you do not have family that can look after your children, ask trusted friends instead. Please don't rationalize never doing it, as you will regret it when your relationship loses its fun and becomes mundane and functional.

If you do not have children, again, work no more than half your time. Make sure your couple time takes up half of the time you don't spend at work, and then socializing can constitute a quarter of your free time, with the rest just for you.

Work	50 per cent
Couple	25 per cent
Socializing	12.5 per cent
Time to self	12.5 per cent.

Following these guidelines will bring back some balance into your life, and ensure that you spend at least some time prioritizing your relationship to keep it going as best you can.

If your partner is resistant to spending more time with you, even at this stage, and in this month when you are trying to heal your relationship, you need to talk to him about it. As calmly as you can, ask him why. Ask him to list his barriers to doing this, remembering your golden rules of communication: the Listening Rules (*see Chapter 3*) and the Talking Rules (*see Chapter 4*).

INJECTING FUN INTO YOUR RELATIONSHIP

When was the last time you did something you absolutely enjoyed, just for yourself? What do you like doing for yourself that you actually make time to do? These sound like ridiculously simple questions but the answer can be harder to give than you think. We often take it as read that we have things we like to do, like going out dancing or playing tennis. But when was the last time you made proper time to do this and invested time in yourself? Moreover, when was the last time you and your partner shared this activity together or did something you really liked to do together?

Fun is not just the cherry on the cake, something frivolous to be guiltily enjoyed once in a while. It is a necessary part of life – doing what you enjoy makes up part of who you are. Think about it: did you get together with your partner to run errands or pay bills? No, this is dull. Were you actually attracted to them because you thought they were dull, or vice versa? No, you were attracted to each other because of the things that make you feel happy and alive and one of these things is usually the capacity for fun.

Case Study | Ian

Ian was a very strong person. When he met his partner it was a case of opposites attracting – they were attracted to how different they were from each other and to the new life experiences they introduced each other to. She loved nature and wildlife and these types of pastime soon became part of Ian's life too. When they first met, he loved more dangerous, adrenalin-based sports which made him feel alive. His partner was deeply attracted to how manly this made him look and would watch him racing his car with pride and a fair amount of lust. However, over the years he spent less and less time doing these sports as his life became more enmeshed with his partner's.

When Ian came to me for help with mild depression six years later, he could not tell me how he identified himself. I asked him to give me three ways he could describe himself to me that were not based on anything physical, e.g. his name, height, hair colour etc. He could not describe himself. Over the years, he had somehow lost his lust for life and excitement, which was such a huge part of his identity. Giving up his interests literally meant he had begun to lose interest in life and himself. Enjoyment is a massive protective factor from things like stress and depression, both for the individual and for a couple. If you enjoy the time you spend together you are more likely to enjoy being together.

Now we've discussed the benefits of quality time, let's look at how you are going to fill it.

🔧 **TASKS FOR BRINGING THE FUN BACK IN**

🕐 These tasks will take 1 day.

Couple's and Individuals' Task

List two activities you like to do, or used to like to do. Then list two things that your partner likes to do, or would like to try. Using the ratio we have already worked out, of when you are going to have some couple time together, book in one of each of these activities for the next month and the other two for the following month.

You are therefore committing to do one thing that you would like to do this month (that is, in the next four weeks) and one thing that your partner would like to do this month, and one thing each in the month that follows (that is, in the next eight weeks). If you are doing this as an individual then you are going to do two things you enjoy each month as you don't have to compromise.

TO SUM UP ...

Over the last three days, you have looked at the ways you can improve your relationship that go beyond verbal communication. You have thought about how you are going to improve your relationship in practical ways, and how you can continue making it as good as it realistically can be from now on.

You have made the decision to become more aware of the way you present yourself verbally and non-verbally, and do this in such a way that ensures you receive respect and kindness. You have also thought about how you can compliment your partner more, so they feel secure.

You have decided to give your relationship enough time to stay happy – this sounds basic, but so many couples forget to prioritize their relationship and expect it to stand the test of time without regular servicing. You have also started to remember that fun for you is also important, rather than always doing what you need to do or prioritizing something or someone else. Lose your sense of fun and you will lose a bit of your identity. Lots of couples complain that the spark and excitement have left their relationship and having fun together is a way of regaining that spark. It is so important to remember to laugh together.

And another important factor is keeping the passion alive ...

CHAPTER 10

SEX AND INTIMACY
Keeping the Flame Alive

Our sex life is a window into the nature of our relationships. It symbolizes the way we feel and function in our relationship, and mirrors the changes that happen with time. So assessing your sex life is like making an assessment of your whole relationship. It is a paradox that the most fascinating topic and the most fundamental and defining aspect of intimate relationships – sex – is the hardest for most couples to talk about.

In spite of its importance, most couples spend more time talking about just about anything else rather than openly communicating about sex. They can joke or argue about sex far more than they can actually discuss it. But if couples cannot talk about sex they cannot really understand how the other perceives their sex life. Then mistrust, lack of confidence and insecurity can develop.

When you're in a relationship with someone, you should be able to just put your bodies together and let each other express what you want from the sexual interaction, simply through how you respond to each other. However, there are so many barriers to this that unless you communicate about it, problems can develop. In fact, it is even important to talk about seemingly healthy sex lives, otherwise there is a danger of becoming increasingly dissatisfied as sexual preferences and fantasies change over time, so you need to keep up.

BRAND-NEW BEGINNINGS

When you first get together, the chances are you are more in lust than anything else. Sex becomes the focus of entire weekends, rather than something you think about doing once a fortnight at midnight. So in the beginning, sex defines our relationships. But this is not realistic or sustainable and, as in anything, focus on one thing does not make for a healthy relationship. As life creeps on, the way we manage our sex lives says a lot about the way we manage our relationships. Once you are both past the lust stage, sex, although still important, stops being the priority of all your free time. As you come out from under the duvet – or each other – you begin to do other things and see other friends again.

THE EARLY STAGE OF A RELATIONSHIP

When you reach this point, it is important that you keep the sexual excitement up and make sure you don't go from one extreme to the other. From 'can't take your hands off each other' to 'forgetting to touch'. If you let this happen, your relationship will very quickly slip purely into friendship, and most likely end soon after with a 'I think we are better off as friends' conversation.

Other couples go to other extremes, such as those who seem to feel they have to demonstrate in public just how hot they are for each other, in the process often offending everyone by being far too publicly sexual in their behaviour. People doing this may think they are giving off 'Aren't we hot and sexy?' vibes, especially if they are supposedly with a group of friends, but more often it is actually a case of 'Aren't we desperate to look hot?' Couples like this are perhaps scared that losing their sexual attraction to each other will mean they lose their relationship, as though sex is all they have. Couples whose relationships follow this pattern tend to be addicted to the first flush of sexual excitement and romance, but once this wears off they lose interest very quickly.

Case Study | Kevin

Kevin was incredibly romantic. When he first met a woman he would figuratively sweep her off her feet. He reported that he was usually part of a couple that could not keep their hands off each other, even when he was out for dinner with friends. He would behave like the most attentive lover – as though he were spellbound by his girlfriend. No romantic gestures were too big. One of his girlfriends returned home to find literally hundreds of beautiful roses and delicious chocolates scattered around her bedroom.

Five months later, he reportedly could not really be bothered to make love to her any more. He thrilled to the idea of wooing a woman, but once his partner began to fall for him and he had 'won the chase', he would lose interest in the idea. He was a classic example of a man who really was thrilled by unfamiliar touch, but once it became familiar it lost all appeal.

BEING IN A RELATIONSHIP, AS OPPOSED TO DATING

Commitment Issues

After your new relationship has survived the first frantic flurry of dating, next comes the issue of commitment. If someone is resistant to commitment, it is usually down to their own issues or expectations of themselves. If you and your partner are in this space, working through the previous chapters will mean you have probably established most of the reasons for this. For instance, when you worked out the underlying reasons why you argue, and pinpointed the core issues (*see Chapter 5*). And hopefully, you will have continued discussing these issues in a rational adult manner.

How Commitment Issues Can Affect Sexual Behaviour

If there is a resistance to settling down, this is sometimes mirrored within the physical side of the relationship. One of you could be resistant to settling down sexually and only having one partner.

A lot of couples who are at this point, but don't want to cheat on each other, engage in swinging or partner swapping, threesomes and the like. Involving other people, sex toys and costumes or role play every time you have sex is a way of avoiding intimacy and real emotional commitment. Now there is nothing wrong with any sexual practice between a consenting couple as long as it does no-one any harm, including the couple. But swinging, or threesomes, can cause massive hurt if one of the couple does not really want to do it and is only consenting in order to keep their partner. This situation reveals a huge power differential in the relationship, with one acting like the passive victim or compliant child (*see Chapters 6 and 7*) and the other like the 'out for all I can get' personality type.

Case Study | Tania and Justin

Tania and Justin lived as swingers. Justin had suggested they try this lifestyle choice two years into their relationship. Tania replied that if they were going to do this she would need to know she was special to him. She wanted to get engaged. Justin reportedly told her he was not ready to make this step yet but he would think about it, and they would talk about it again in six months.

At first, they tended to couple-swap with other couples. The women would have sex together while the men would have sex with the two women, but not with each other. Tania felt quite secure with this. She enjoyed the sex and felt that although other people were involved in their sex lives, it was okay because it was another couple. She still felt important to Justin and 'on his team'. But Justin wanted to add more variety, and soon another single girl was regularly joining them. This pushed the boundaries of the sex into an orgy. Before long, their relationship became a threesome. The new girl, Izzie, started to spend all of her time with them. Not just joining them for sex but also for dinner, watching TV, everything. Justin had effectively set himself up with two girlfriends.

Izzie and Tania apparently became best friends, but deep down Tania obviously felt intense jealousy. She realized that she was now in a competition with the other girl and Justin was the prize. She also finally realized that he was not even that special, and certainly not worth living a life that made her so deeply unhappy. Tania had wanted a partner so much that she blurred her sexual boundaries for him. This developed into a blurring of her lifestyle boundaries and massively decreased her self-esteem.

Tania and Justin initially came to see me because Tania's low self-esteem was affecting her confidence sexually, which annoyed Justin as it affected his *ménage-à-trois*. Eventually Tania admitted to herself that she did not want to keep being so sexually adventurous. She wanted to love and be loved by someone and to make love, not have orgies and apparent sexual adventure. Tania left Justin, who went on to live with Izzie and together they totally immersed themselves in the swinging lifestyle. As Tania recovered from the relationship she also had to recover and deal with the psychological consequences of a sex life that felt to her now almost similar to abuse. Although she had consented to the situation, she had forced herself to do this to keep Justin, rather than doing it for her own sexual excitement or enjoyment. Luckily for her she realized he was not worth her tears or remorse and she could move on and find her perfect type of relationship.

I am not condemning this lifestyle choice. But you do have to be clear that you are really consenting to it, and not consenting just to keep your partner, which so many people end up doing. In fact, with all the swingers I have worked with, one partner has always secretly been ashamed of their choice and not really enjoyed it. It is something they are doing to keep their partner. This is absolutely not healthy and an example of how sexual choices can be really damaging to a relationship. But then, happy couples don't walk into my therapy rooms.

BORED BY BEING A COUPLE?

If your sexual relationship always has to involve other people, or involves other people more often than one of you would like, or when you only get seriously excited when you are joined by a third person, this shows a serious problem between you. As with everything, balance is healthy. If you both like threesomes but equally like just the two of you, then this can be healthy. However, if you are sexually bored by just the two of you, you need to focus on spicing up just the two of you – without anyone else first. If in order to have a fulfilling sex life you need to bring others in, ultimately you will not feel content, as deep down every couple knows that if they can't get turned on by their partner alone then they are not really happy and unrest will be niggling away at them.

Case Study | Elaine and Chris

Elaine and Chris apparently kept their passion alive by having threesomes. This seemed to be what they both wanted. They alternated by having threesomes with another man for her, and with another woman for him. Now, on the surface this looked like a couple making sure the excitement stayed alive in their relationship. However, psychologically it is not that healthy to be able to share your partner sexually without jealousy; and also to only have sex when someone else is there. It isn't keeping it alive, it's taking over. Elaine and Chris kept telling me they could both do this. They were so secure that this did not bother them. But they also displayed signs of not worrying when they did not see each other much at all, and their quality time alone was clearly not a priority to either of them, just as quality sexual interactions alone were not a priority.

Basically, they wanted each other in their lives because they enjoyed having someone there. A lot of the things they did were functional – they had quality 'at home' evenings but distracted themselves by watching films and never talking. Further, Chris was apparently proud of how they could socialize so well at parties, but in reality this ability to stand alone and talk to others, rather than hanging off each other, was a desire to talk to anyone but each other. Again, balance is key, some time together, some apart.

And their sex life was the most obvious manifestation of this: they both wanted to have sex with other people and having threesomes was a way of doing this without theoretically cheating on each other. They liked each other, but were not in love or fascinated by each other. They were two insecure people that needed to feel as though they were in love, so they found each other and constructed a relationship that looked good on paper, but was without any strong emotional bond.

FANTASIZING ABOUT OTHERS

To a lesser degree, this is true of having fantasies about other people when you are making love to your partner. You love them but wish they were physically different, or you are just bored constantly making love to them. Some fantasy is normal, but constant fantasy – like any extreme – can be damaging, as it stops you really appreciating each other sexually. If you have a tendency to do this, try to fantasize, at most, for 50 per cent of the time, and during the other 50 per cent enjoy what you and your partner have together.

MOVING IN TOGETHER

Think about when your relationship moved up a life stage (if it already has). Did you maintain a sex life or were you more turned on by your soft furnishings than each other? Did you become so house-proud you could only relax enough to have sex if the house, or at least the room you were going to make love in, was spotless? Did you become more interested in setting up house with each other than in each other? If so, this is an indication that you are beginning to represent a role to each other – that you or your partner is a key into adult domesticity, rather than people with a close emotional and physical connection. If you and your partner are focusing on domestic arrangements to the exclusion of the rest of your relationship, it could be a ruse to hide the fact that you are not enough for each other on your own.

Case Study | Mia and Tom

As I have already mentioned, Mia and Tom lived in a lovely house, which they both took great pride in setting up. Indeed, they told me that setting up home together was the time they felt closest to each other. Of course they did – they had a shared project that fascinated them, which compensated for the fact that they were not that fascinated by each other. They felt close because they had a shared passion and that passion was not their relationship, it was their house.

They were also very interested in showing they had status and wealth, therefore they were more interested in doing up their house incredibly stylishly than in each other. They would rather spend a fortune on a sofa than a holiday for just the two of them. Yes, you can argue this rationally: a sofa lasts longer and is a more practical use of money. But in their case, what this really showed was that a holiday – time with just the two of them did not interest them as much as a luxurious leather sofa. They were getting so bored by each other that they actually found furniture more interesting.

But, as in all things, they thought they had a great relationship at this point. Just as they thought their house was incredibly fashionable, so they described their sex lives. They experimented with lots of different sex toys, never with other people; it was the toys they were into. They always tried the latest toys. This can be a very sexually rewarding experience – to share sex and sex toys to give each other lots of pleasure – but again, only in balance. Sometimes sex needs to be just the two of you, with no barriers or accessories. It needs to be just two souls and bodies intertwined, rather than a biological project to always pursue the maximum climax. Balance is key: sometimes being sexually adventurous, sometimes making love in a way that connects mind, body and soul. In the case of Mia and Tom, the fact that they needed the sex toys to get excited only further revealed that they needed a distraction from each other sexually, as well as in the rest of their life. Sex toys had become a way of avoiding intimacy.

LONG-TERM RELATIONSHIPS AND BEYOND

There is no doubt that a familiar touch becomes less exciting over time, and when life creeps in or takes over our sex lives can pay the price.

Having a Family

Having children has a massive effect on your sex life and your relationship – if you let it. Women who have given birth to their children (rather than adopt or go through surrogacy) often feel as though their bodies are now more maternal than sexual. This has obvious links to pregnancy and childbirth, and is particularly true in the first year if the woman is breastfeeding. However, with the right psychological approach it is possible for the woman to see herself as having shared her body with her children for a short time, rather than lost control and sexual ownership of it completely.

Case Study | Sarah

Sarah had always taken a pride in her figure. She had been in a sexually unfulfilling marriage for five years, where she could only manage the sexual act by fantasizing about being with someone else. (This is a common use of fantasy – to enable you to have sex with someone you cannot make yourself attracted to any more, and is a huge sign your relationship is in crisis.) When her marriage finally broke down, she met a new partner with whom she shared a fantastic sex life, and this developed into an intense relationship where she became pregnant after a year.

During her pregnancy she made an effort to stay glamorous – more for her own self-image than to please her partner. They continued to have a great sex life, and the two of them stayed emotionally and physically connected. After the baby was born, she breastfed but also used bottles with expressed breast milk in them so she could feel like a woman and not a milk dispenser (her words). She started having sex again when she wanted to, on the condition that her partner did the night-time feeds so she was not always exhausted. They negotiated a way for her to get back to being a woman as well as a mum, by him being a very hands-on father. Although she was an excellent mother, Sarah did not become an invisible, asexual woman. She had made a conscious decision to prioritize the sexual side of her identity, as well as taking on the identity of a new mum.

WHEN SEX BECOMES A CHORE

Young children running around can be very sexually inhibiting. Indeed, the stress of creating a new family comes at time when you need a close connection with your partner more than ever. This is not the time to start drifting apart, and sexual interactions, it does not always have to be intercourse, will contribute to keeping a relationship close. However, too many partners go through the motions. They grant sex to keep the other happy, like a monthly treat, rather than because they need it and it excites them.

You can avoid this unsatisfying scenario by keeping your psychological and physical interest up. Keep in touch with what turns you on in bed and make it an experience on your terms. Which brings us back to asking for what you want. Start to think about sex less in terms of keeping your partner happy for a while, and more in terms of something that would really give you pleasure. Then make sure you find a way of communicating this desire to your partner – they will benefit from it as much as you will.

Sharing the Workload

If this sounds exhausting, then maybe your partner needs to get up with the children in the night more often, regardless of who works outside the home. Working in the home is work too. Of the couples with whom I have worked those who seem to get this balance the best tend to be gay men who have adopted, and gay women. Obviously I am not advocating that in order to share childcare arrangements you need to be in a gay relationship, but I am saying that in order to really share you have to try to ignore and dismiss stereotypical societal expectations. I think gay relationships tend to manage this better because there are less common stereotypical societal expectations attached.

Let me explain what I mean. As a society we seem to have very definite views on what makes a good or bad mother. Although we now have the stereotype of 'yummy mummies' – another difficult ideal for women to live up to! – we rarely see being sexual as part of what makes a good mother. So if women are to become great earth mothers, the other aspects of their beings get ignored.

For gay couples it is different. There is no model of what makes a good father in a gay relationship, or whether the women should take on the traditional 'male' or 'female' roles. So these couples tend to add parenthood on to the rest of their identity, rather than making their mother or father role the whole thing, a very healthy way of incorporating parenthood. They are good parents, but they tend to remember the rest of their identity as well.

What we can all learn from this is that we are a couple, as well as parents. And as a couple, you should both prioritize this. If the father never does the night feeds or never gets up at the crack of dawn with the children, he is not making his relationship – as part of a supportive and sexual couple – a priority. If the mother has to do all the exhausting aspects of the childcare, she simply becomes too tired to think about anything else at all, especially sex.

LET'S TALK ABOUT SEX

Long-term relationships need to keep sex exciting and yes,

you will need to work harder at it. The key to this, as I have already intimated throughout this chapter, just as with everything else, is communication.

The following case studies are examples of how miscommunication can affect even the most established of sexual relationships.

Case Study | One

A woman yawns and stretches and heads for bed at 8.30pm, saying to her husband, 'Coming to bed, dear?' Her husband glances at the TV and mumbles, 'Going to bed so early?' 'Yes, I am really tired. Aren't you?' 'No. I'll be right up after the news. Sleep well.' 'Oh, all right then.' This undemonstrative conversation actually contained a sexual invitation, albeit an insecure one, to a husband who often complained about the low frequency of sex in his marriage.

Case Study | Two

Bill complains bitterly to his wife that their sex life is too pedestrian. They are in a rut and he would like to try something other than the missionary position. He suggests they trying having sex 'front to back'. His wife immediately thinks he does not find her attractive any more, and that he is never going to want to look at her during sex again. She begins to cry that he expects too much from her. Bill does not like to see his wife cry. He loves her, so he comforts her, and is effectively silenced from discussing his sexual needs. Bill suffers in silence while his wife broods that he is not happy with their sex life, and they end up having sex even less because they cannot talk about it.

Case studies adapted from *Messages: The Communication Skills Book*, McKay, Davis and Fanning, 1983. Oakland, CA: New Harbinger Publications.

Case Study | Three

A couple judge themselves too much during sex. Rather than just enjoying the moment, they worry about their performance and how pleasing it is to the other. They do not say anything about this to each other, they just worry quietly to themselves. Because they cannot talk about it, they cannot take away all their thoughts. They cannot just let their feelings control their body and its movements. Indeed, because they are judging themselves so much they each remain in their heads and do not let themselves connect with their bodies. This means they cannot express what they want simply through where they place their limbs.

They forget to ask themselves what they want and just think about how they are doing. They forget about sexual connection and obsess instead about giving a perfectly executed performance. They worry so much about how they look – concentrating on sucking in their tummy, making sure they hide their cellulite – that they stop their brains and bodies communicating together and so neither ends up having a sexually satisfactory experience.

SEXUAL MYTHS

Myths about what a healthy sex life is often prevent a couple from broaching the subject of changes in their sex life. The three main myths are:

- You should not have to talk about sex with your partner because sex will naturally take care of itself.

- Your partner should be considerate and sensitive enough to know how to sexually satisfy you.

- You should avoid conflict at all costs. It would be terrible to ask your partner something and be refused.

  (From *Messages: The Communication Skills Book*, McKay, Davis and Fanning, 1983. Oakland, CA: New Harbinger Publications.)

As you are a complex human being, your sex life is much more than a natural biological process. As we discussed earlier, it is keenly sensitive to psychological factors. Life changes, your personal beliefs, your past sexual experiences, current stressors and other preoccupations will all affect your sex life. This makes it even more important to tune into what you are thinking, feeling and wanting sexually, so that you keep up with these changes and communicate your sexual needs and thoughts to your partner openly. The more open you both are, the more likely you are to receive support and cooperation.

Why should you expect your partner to be a mind reader? Unless you tell them how you feel and what you would like, they can't know. It is no reflection on the sexual prowess of either of you to have to talk about what you want. If your partner is not satisfying you, it is probably not because they don't care enough to try. It is more likely to be because you haven't been sufficiently open about what you both want. Or maybe you have told them what you want, but you have not let them respond with how they really feel about it.

People often feel guilty about talking about what they want sexually, as though they are somehow criticizing their partner. Guilt further distorts communication – you may be worried about coming across as critical, which makes you too defensive. Then your defensiveness is met by more defensiveness and effective communication is prevented.

DOING WHAT FEELS RIGHT FOR BOTH OF YOU

Everyone has the right to refuse a sexual request, but it is always a good idea to first really discuss it with your partner. They may be refusing to do something because of 'What if?' fantasies that they are not voicing to you. You may have asked for oral sex and they could be thinking, 'What if I can't do it right? My partner will laugh at me ...' But rather than admitting this they say, 'No, I don't like the idea.' The truth is not that they don't like the idea, but that they are worried they'll make a fool of themselves.

Everyone, and I do mean everyone, has some sexual insecurities. But if you talk through why you are asking for something, and your partner talks through how they really feel about it, perhaps you can both get to a happy resolution.

So in the case study I described earlier involving Justin and Tania, she should have explored the fact she was only agreeing to the threesomes because of her 'What if?' fantasy. 'What if he leaves me if I don't do what he wants?'

Justin would probably have agreed that he might leave her, as he was so desperate to have sex with others. Then Tania could have realized that she should refuse. It would have been obvious that Justin was not really asking her to do this to enhance their sexual relationship, but because he did not really want her any more.

⚒ THE GOLDEN RULES OF SEXUAL COMMUNICATION

- Check in with yourself first. Be clear about what you want and what you need to change.

- Check your partner is in as good a mood as any to discuss this topic. After a stressful day, or at two in the morning, would usually not be a good time.

- Be positive. Don't say, 'You rub me too hard, I want you to stop it. I hate it.' Instead say, 'I'd enjoy it more if you were to try to rub me more gently.'

- Start with 'I' so you are taking responsibility for your need. Say, 'I need you to connect with me more during sex,' rather than, 'You clearly can't climax if you think about me and your fantasizing is really hurting me.' This places blame on the other person and will only be met by defensiveness.

- Be specific. If you want to try outdoor sex then say so. Don't coyly say, 'Let's be more adventurous,' as this goes back to assuming some degree of mind-reading.

- Make sure you actively listen to your partner in return. Check what your partner has taken from what you have actually said. Try to find out how they have interpreted what you have just said, or what they think you said. As everyone can be insecure around this issue they may have taken your suggestion for more excitement as a criticism of your current sex life. Make sure they understand that it is not.

- Stay on the topic. If your partner gets defensive and comes back with, 'Well, you don't give me enough oral sex either,' respond with, 'Well, we can talk about that afterwards but can we just hear me first.' One couple got so defensive and so off the point that what started out as a request for more sex out of the bedroom turned into a discussion on who did the most washing-up!

- Agree on how you are going to try and experiment with the new idea.

- Agree to talk about it afterwards to see how you both felt about it.

- Thank your partner for talking about this as you know it can be a very sensitive topic.

- Don't talk too much about your problems or make mountains out of molehills. A one-off lost erection due to stress does not merit a complete re-evaluation of your sex life.

✎ TASKS FOR SPICING UP YOUR SEX LIFE

🕐 These tasks will take 4 days.

👥👤 *Couple's and Individuals' Tasks*

List the beliefs and fears that you may have about discussing your sex life with your sexual partner.

Share your lists, if currently in a relationship, following the above golden rules, so you can be aware of the issues you each might have when it comes to talking about sex. Try and reassure each other as you go along.

DAY 29

👥 *Couple's Task*

Together, list any external stressors that currently inhibit your sex life. Decide on strategies to overcome them.

For instance:

Stressor	Strategy
Baby in cot next to bed	Have sex in kitchen when children asleep.
Always too tired	Have a weekend away together, just the two of you, without work or responsibilities. Go to a hotel to relax and eat, drink and

make love, not to sightsee, once every other month.

 Individuals' Task

Decide what you would like to change about your sex life in your future relationships. Distinguish between the sex life you have as someone out of a relationship and the sex you have as someone in a relationship. Let's face it, if you are having brief sexual liaisons right now you will have different priorities than if you were in a committed relationship. Make a list of changes you plan to make generally to improve your sex life, then start to consider strategies for how you are going to bring these changes about. The next task helps with this.

DAY 30

Couple's and Individuals' Task

Think back to whether there was ever a time when your sex life felt better. If so, talk about what was different and think about how you can bring this back.

For example:

Sex was better because	What we can do
Had sex more regularly	Go to bed together five times a week, not two, so one of you does not always stay up later.

Don't do tasks or work before going to bed. Unwind for a moment on your own so you are more relaxed and in the mood.

| Had sex in bath more | Have sex in bath again! |

DAY 31

Finally, let's get in touch with your fantasies, as they have a crucial and important part in any sex life. Fantasies shared, even if it is just verbally, can be very exciting.

In order to get in touch with your fantasies, think about your wildest sexual daydreams. What are the recurring themes? Surprise, romance, slow undressing, oral sex, submission/dominance, outdoor sex, groups?

While some of these might not be things you actually want to do, you might just want to pretend, so try mentally bringing them into your sex life. Talk about how people are watching you while you are having sex. In some cases talking dirty about it will bring nearly the same excitement as actually doing it, and without the fear of arrest. Some of the fantasies you might actually want to carry out, so decide which ones you are going to try. But remember the pitfalls we saw earlier in the chapter if you do this, and make sure you are both happy about what you are doing.

Be Fair

When acting out fantasies, make sure you each have your fair share. So if you are doing three of your partner's, then you should also always do three of yours. There should never be any unfairness surrounding your fantasies. This would only cause resentment.

TO SUM UP ...

In this chapter we have discussed why it is so important for you to communicate with your partner about your sex life and how this will lead to deeper intimacy. I have given you some golden rules on how to do this and we have also looked at some of the blocks to communication.

We have also seen what your sex life can tell you about latent problems in your relationship. This should help you to think about how you can heal any problems both in your sexual and in your everyday relationship. Finally, the tasks in this chapter were geared to encouraging you to think about how you can have a more fun, adventurous and exciting sex life together. Enjoy.

CHAPTER II

THE END OF YOUR JOURNEY
Moving On From Here

Congratulations! You have almost made it to the end of your journey to heal your relationship. As a final consolidation of all your work, I would like to quickly recap the steps of your journey:

BEING TRUE TO YOURSELF

All the work you have done so far has been aimed at helping you to become someone who values being authentic, rather than someone who is always playing a role or trying to be someone they are not, in their relationships.

LEARNING TO TRUST

At the same time, you should now be able both to trust your partner and to be trusted by them. Think about the task you did where you led your blindfolded partner, and were led blindfold by your partner; this idea should not worry you at all any more.

Becoming Self-Reliant

If you have been taking this journey through the book on your own, and working on the individual tasks, you should be able to see now how you can rely on yourself and trust yourself to make sure your next relationship is the best possible relationship for you. Now you have much more trust in yourself, you can be confident that you can rely on your own judgements, and this will hold true whether you are part of a couple or not. Knowing you have this self-reliance means you don't need to panic about things that would ordinarily faze you, you should no longer feel so defensive that you think you have to fight your corner. Now you are free to live a life that suits you, calmly and rationally.

Breaking Free of Arguments

This self-reliance should herald the end of hysterical arguments, especially if you also keep in mind the tasks we explored when we examined the argument rut. As we discovered, when we argue a lot we can feel that our relationships are fake. We may look happy on the outside, but the mess behind the door can be overwhelming. You should be free of this mess by now, not only because you trust each other, or are at least working towards trusting each other, on a daily basis, but also because you genuinely know how to avoid arguments.

Finding Out Your 'Core Issues'

The other crucial factor we explored in Chapter 5 was how to stop arguing about the 'symptoms' of your core issues, rather than the real problems themselves. So instead of arguing about activities you'll be doing at the weekend, you can get straight to the point by letting your partner know that you feel they don't always make you their top priority. Learning to recognize these 'core issues' really is a breakthrough point in your relationships – and that includes all your relationships, such as those with family and work colleagues too – as it will cut through a lot of unnecessary angst.

Learning to Communicate

The reason you can talk to each other in a more honest and respectful way is because you have now started following the **Golden Rules of Communication**. Following these rules means you can be assertive and take ownership of your thoughts, feelings and needs. So you can both talk without blaming each other or getting defensive.

Being Aware of Personality Types

In the next stage of the process, we focused Chapters 6 and 7 on remembering (or discovering!) who you and your partner really are, and how the dynamics of your interactions work. In other words, what your personality types are and how they can complement each other in some areas and rub each other up the wrong way in others.

Remembering Who You Are

Whether you were doing this on your own or as part of a couple, I hope you will always try to remember who you can be when you are being yourself. Also, that you realize that the insecure, moaning Minnie or Michael you might sometimes have become is the direct result of how insecure you were feeling in the relationship – perhaps because of the type of person your partner is, or because your behaviour has not encouraged them to be reassuring. But once you change *your* own behaviour, you will start to remember who you are and how you would like to be treated in a relationship. Once you've got that right, you'll find the moaning Minnie is a person of the past.

Acting Like an Adult

Linked to being true to yourself is the work you have done on being a rational, authentic, and grounded adult. Hopefully, you have now banished the critical or nurturing parent, and the rebellious or compliant child, to only 2 per cent of your behaviour (no-one is perfect, so you are never going to behave like an adult 100 per cent of the time, especially when it is one in the morning and you are drunk, tired and emotional, and your partner wants one more drink – or, perhaps, one more game of poker!).

Remembering to Have (Adult!) Fun

Seriously, though, I hope that by working through this book you have realized that behaving like an adult does not mean being dull. In fact, it means the opposite. When you are being a rational adult you can have pure, unadulterated fun without the drama or heartache of it all going wrong. Without fear of the childish ego state metaphorically or literally stamping its foot and ruining what was actually a great night out.

The rational adult also helps you get what you need out of a relationship, whether that's as serious as actual commitment and finally moving in together after four years, or something as seemingly trivial but annoying as help with the washing-up. The rational adult does this, because if you act like you deserve something others begin to think you do too.

Practical Life Skills

I have also given you some life skills to help maintain these changes. These life skills are about how you communicate to your partner the type of relationship you want, without using words, by using body language, confidence, and acting as if you deserve respect.

We also looked at how important it is to value yourself, and to set yourself up for your day in the right frame of mind. Remember the task I gave you to talk to yourself in the mirror. Somewhat embarrassing at first, I'm sure! But, as you learnt, actually giving yourself a compliment in the mirror each morning helps you start the day feeling as though someone has been nice to you – even if it is yourself. In fact, most things are better when you are being nice to yourself; by now you should be able to give the best compliments to yourself.

Hopefully, while you were working through the tasks that remind you to be true to yourself, you also remembered what you like to do, and you have also started doing things that make you happy. You should by now have two great things planned to do in the next eight weeks. I hope you enjoy them.

Revving Up Your Sex Life

Last, but by no means least, I hope you have improved the quality of your sex life. And while we were at it, perhaps the quantity too. Fantasy, excitement, and passion should at least be back on the agenda, if not completely back in your current sex life. The key to all this, as I keep on saying throughout the book, is communication. No-one is a mind-reader, least of all during sex. Just as in the rest of your life, you get the sex you want by asking for it in a way that encourages agreement from your partner, rather than having them running for the hills, muttering 'Weirdo!' as they go.

BEFORE WE GO ...

So in order to check that you are where you should be, I'd like you to do exactly what I would do with you if you were sitting opposite me in my consulting room. I'd like you to return to your original list of what needs changing. Find the list you wrote on Day 1. This task was for individuals as well as couples, so I want you to look at it just from your perspective, regardless of whether your partner is doing this with you or not.

Have you addressed everything you need to? Can you see how these problem areas will change with your new style of thinking and acting within your relationship? If you were sitting with me now, and you had retained all of this information and made the necessary changes, the problems you were having should be pretty much eliminated. Remember we are not aiming for the impossible – perfection – here, but we should be able to tick those issues off your list as a job well done.

CELEBRATE YOUR ACHIEVEMENT

So now all that remains is to give yourself big congratulations. You are now leaving this therapy well on the way to having a fixed relationship. This has happened because you have worked really hard at achieving it. All the improvements are down to you. You have worked through this book and deserve credit for doing so. You should be feeling so much happier now and you deserve to be.

And remember that if there are things that are still not quite right, the biggest step is always the first one, and that is simply to identify them. Then return to the relevant tasks and re-do them until things are right. You will get there in the end, so don't despair. Everyone works at a different pace and some people just need a bit longer than others. There is no harm in this at all.

Meanwhile, take stock of how far you have come. Be proud of yourselves and make sure you do something to celebrate. Pour yourself (and your partner, if you have one) a lovely glass of wine or champagne and be as good and kind to yourself and each other as you can. You know you really are worth it – congratulations.

Titles of Related Interest

Dawn Breslin's Guide to SuperConfidence, by Dawn Breslin

Everything I've Ever Learned About Love, by Lesley Garner

The Law of Attraction, by Esther and Jerry Hicks

Love Yourself ... and It Doesn't Matter Who You Marry, by Eva-Maria Zurhorst

The Power of Intention, by Dr Wayne W. Dyer

You Can Have What You Want, by Michael Neill

You Can Heal Your Life, by Louise L. Hay

We hope you enjoyed this Hay House book.
If you would like to receive a free catalogue featuring additional
Hay House books and products, or if you would like information
about the Hay Foundation, please contact:

Hay House UK Ltd
Unit B • 292 Kensal Road • London W10 5BE
Tel: (44) 20 8962 1230; Fax: (44) 20 8962 1239
www.hayhouse.co.uk

****

Published and distributed in the United States of America by:
Hay House, Inc. • P.O. Box 5100 • Carlsbad, CA 92018-5100
Tel: (1) 760 431 7695 or (800) 654 5126; Fax: (1) 760 431 6948 or (800) 650 5115
www.hayhouse.com

****

Published and distributed in Australia by:
Hay House Australia Ltd • 18/36 Ralph St • Alexandria NSW 2015
Tel: (61) 2 9669 4299 • Fax: (61) 2 9669 4144
www.hayhouse.com.au

****

Published and distributed in the Republic of South Africa by:
Hay House SA (Pty) Ltd • PO Box 990 • Witkoppen 2068
Tel/Fax: (27) 11 706 6612 • orders@psdprom.co.za

****

Distributed in Canada by:
Raincoast • 9050 Shaughnessy St • Vancouver, BC V6P 6E5
Tel: (1) 604 323 7100 • Fax: (1) 604 323 2600

****

Sign up via the Hay House UK website to receive the Hay House
online newsletter and stay informed about what's going on with
your favourite authors. You'll receive bimonthly announcements
about discounts and offers, special events, product highlights,
free excerpts, giveaways, and more!

www.hayhouse.co.uk